M000198414

Against Equality

queer critiques of gay marriage

Against Equality is art and publishing collective dispersed across the United States and Canada. Together we manage an online archive of critical texts devoted to queer and trans critiques of the neoliberal mainstream gay and lesbian politics of inclusion. These texts focus on gay marriage, gays in the military and hate crimes legislation.

This archive can be accessed online at

www.againstequality.org

Against Equality

queer critiques of gay marriage

Edited by Ryan Conrad

Published by:

Against Equality Publishing Collective, 8 Howe Street, Lewiston ME 04240.

Cover design by:

Chris Vargas - www.chrisevargas.com

Dedicated to all the queer and trans folks
engaged in the desperate search for our
most fantastic queer histories...

CONTENTS

Acknowledgements

This project would not have been possible without the endless hours of writing and editing done by all our contributors and those that continue to take a chance on publish our work. Many thanks to UltraViolet, The Bilerico Project, QueerCents, Maximum Rocknroll, the Gay and Lesbian Review, South End Press, AK Press, and the numerous personal blogs on which our work has been posted and re-posted.

Against Equality, Against Marriage: An Introduction
Yasmin Nair

A Progress Narrative

The history of gay marriage supposedly goes something like this: In the beginning, gay people were horribly oppressed. Then came the 1970s, where gays—all of whom looked like the men of The Village People— were able to live openly and have a lot of sex. Then, in the 1980s, many gay people died of AIDS—because they had too much sex in the 1970s. This taught them that gay sex is bad. The gays who were left realized the importance of stable, monogamous relationships and began to agitate for marriage and the 1000+ benefits it would bring. Soon, in the very near future, with the help of supportive, married straight people—and President Obama—gays will gain marriage rights in all 50 states, and they will then be as good and productive as everyone else.

This is, obviously, a reductive and, yes, tongue-in-cheek history. But it is also, sadly, exactly the reductive history that circulates in both the straight and gay media. In a 2009 column commemorating the 40th anniversary of the Stonewall riots, the liberal Frank Rich of *The New York Times* described the events thus: "The younger gay men—and scattered women—who acted up at the Stonewall on those early summer nights in 1969 had little in common with their contemporaries in the front-page political movements of the time." Rich ignored, willfully or not, the fact that Stonewall was initiated largely by unruly drag queens and transgender people, the sort who would have been avoided by the "gay men" who achieve such prominence in his sanitized version of gay history, one that reads like something from the press offices of the conservative National Gay and Lesbian Task Force (NGLTF) or the ultra-conservative Human Rights Campaign (HRC). Rich went on to draw an arc directly from Stonewall to the contemporary gay rights movement, as if its history were simply an upwards movement towards marriage. He even made the outrageous claim that AIDS was made much worse because those who struggled with the disease and were activists in the period were people "whose abridged rights made them even more vulnerable during a rampaging plague." In other words, if only they had the rights bestowed upon them by marriage, gays would not have suffered quite so much.

Rich concluded that "…full gay citizenship is far from complete." By that, of course, he meant that only marriage could guarantee "full" citizenship. He dismissed the complexity of gay history (which did not begin with Stonewall) and ignored the fact that much of gay liberation was founded on leftist and feminist principles, which included a strong materialist critique of marriage. Or that AIDS activism in the 1980s called for universal health care, the demand for which has been abandoned by the gay mainstream in favor of the idea that gays should simply be given health care via marriage.

Rich's views are widely echoed in a world where the default liberal/progressive/left position on gay marriage is an uncritical and ahistorical support of it as a magic pill that will cure all the ills facing contemporary gays/queers. 2008 saw a spate of suicides by teens who killed themselves after relentless bullying by peers for supposedly being gay. This led straights and gays alike to assert that the legalization of gay marriage would remove the stigma of being gay by conferring normality upon queer/queer-identified teens. Gay marriage would supposedly prevent such tragic moments. But if we follow this idea to its logical end, it becomes apparent that what appears to be a wish to bestow dignity upon queers is in fact deeply rooted in a fear and loathing of the unmarried and a neoliberal belief that the addition of private rights tied to the state's munificence will end all social problems.

In a December 2009 blog for *The Nation* titled "On the New York Senate Marriage Equality Vote," Melissa Harris-Lacewell wrote about the extreme harassment suffered by her lesbian niece at her school, which eventually led to her transferring out. Bizarrely, Harris-Lacewell connected the lack of "marriage equality" to her niece's troubles: "Each time we refuse to recognize LGBT persons as first class citizens, deserving of all the rights and protections of the state, we make the world more harsh, more dangerous, and more difficult for my niece and for all gay and transgender young people. They deserve better." On the way to this strange formulation, she conceded that "marriage equality" will not solve the systemic problems of violence and institutional discrimination, but on this she was firm: "marriage equality" would make life better and easier for LGBTs. What is so puzzling is that Harris is purportedly on the left and writes for a magazine whose leftist credentials are well established.

Yet, surely, if a teen is unhappy or commits suicide because he/she is gay and cannot bear to live in a homophobic world, or because he/she is relentlessly taunted by peers for looking/acting gay, surely the problem, the very great problem, lies in the shocking cruelty of a world that will not tolerate any deviation from a norm. When we decide that the solution to such cruelty is to ensure that queer/queer-seeming teens should appear normal via gay marriage, are we not explicitly condoning and even creating a world where discrimination is acceptable? Are we not explicitly telling queer teens and adults that non-conformity can and should lead to death?

Whose Equality? At What Cost?

Such convoluted pieces of logic overdetermine today's relentless quest for gay marriage, a quest that is portrayed in terms of an attainment of "full citizenship" (begging the question: who has half citizenship, exactly?) and in terms of "full equality." But who gains "equality" under these circumstances? And at what cost? One of the biggest arguments for gay marriage is that it would allow gays and lesbians to access the over 1000 benefits that straight married people can access. Well-known feminists like Gloria Steinem give their stamp of approval to gay marriage with the rationale that "we" (feminists) have changed marriage for the better. Yet, while it may be true that women can no longer be raped by their husbands with impunity, the basic nature of marriage is unchanged: it remains the neoliberal state's most efficient way to corral the family as a source of revenue and to place upon it the ultimate responsibility for guaranteeing basic benefits like health care. Furthermore, if millions of people are excluded from the 1000+ benefits simply because they are NOT married, surely it does not matter that "we" have changed the institution when we now choose to ignore the inequalities perpetuated by marriage? Surely we ought not to be for a society where basic benefits like health care are only granted to those who get married? Surely the point is not to change an archaic institution but to change, you know, the world?

The history of gay marriage is now used to overwrite all of queer history as if the gay entrance into that institution were a leap into modernity, as if marriage is all that queers have ever aspired to, as if everything we have wrought and seen and known were all towards this one goal. Americans are fond of judging modernity in the Islamic world by the extent to which women there are allowed to toss away their veils. In the U.S landscape of "gay rights," marriage is the veil: the last barrier between gays and lesbians and "full citizenship." Opening it up to them is considered the last sign of gay modernity, still to be attained. Liberals and lefties alike, straight and gay, look at gay marriage in countries like Spain and Argentina as the ultimate mark of civilization. They note approvingly that South Africa guarantees a constitutional right to gay marriage, but they have nothing to say about the fact that the same country has over 5 million people living with HIV and no similar guarantee for health care.

Gay marriage is seen as the core of a new kind of privatized and personal endeavor—the rights of LGBT *individuals* to enter into a private contract. This ignores the fact that the US is the only major industrialized nation to tie so many basic benefits like health care to marriage. Gay marriage advocates are fond of pointing to Norway or Canada as prime examples of countries where gay marriage is legal, as examples to emulate. They ignore one basic fact: in all these countries, citizens were guaranteed rights like health care long before they legislated marriage. Simply put: in Canada, getting divorced does not put you at risk of losing your health care and dying from a treatable condition. I am not suggesting Canada's public health program is perfect and not under constant threat from the conservative Harper regime, but the fact is that health care is not a basic right in the United States. Tiny differences, but extreme consequences.

Over the same period of years that the gay marriage fight has gathered steam, roughly two and a half decades, the US has also slid into an increasingly fragile economic state. Over 45 million Americans are uninsured (the new health care "reform" is likely to prove too onerous for most). On the queer front, we have seen an increase in the policing, surveillance and arrests in cases of displays of public sexuality, made especially resonant in the recent case of DeFarra Gaymon, who was shot to death by the police in a park in Newark, supposedly during an undercover sting operation and while supposedly engaging in public sex. HIV/AIDS rates are not only rising, those infected with the virus are now among the newly criminalized. A dearth of funds is causing the closure of resources and safe spaces for queer homeless youth.

This anthology is impelled by the failure of both the gay rights movement and a so-called left to address the nightmare of neoliberalism that faces us today. We see this as the moment to move beyond the idea that marriage could ever be part of a radical vision for change. These essays, by writers, activists, and academics on the left, highlight the harmful role of marriage in a neoliberal state that emphasizes issues of identity and the family in order to deflect attention away from the attrition of social services and benefits. Focusing on the family as the arbiter of benefits also ignores the fact that the exclusion of queer people from the normative family structure is marked by physical and psychological violence. When queers criticize the State's emphasis on the normative family, we do so because we know only too well the violence of exclusion and because, for many of us, our identities as queer people have been marked and shaped, not always in unproductive ways, by that violence.

In short, the family is the best way to advance capitalism, as the base unit through which capitalism distributes benefits. Through our reliance on the marital family structure, emphasized and valorized by the push for gay marriage, we allow the state to mandate that only some relationships and some forms of social networks count. If you are married, you get health care. If you are not, go and die on your sad and lonely deathbed by yourself; even the state will not take care of you. If you are married, you get to be the good immigrant and bring over your immediate and extended family to set up a family business and send your children to the best schools after years of perseverance and hard work (at least theoretically). If you are not, you can be deported and imprisoned at the slightest infraction and not one of the kinship networks that you are a part of will count in the eyes of the state. In other words, a queer radical critique of the family is not simply the celebration of an outsider status, although it is often that, but an economic critique. A queer radical critique of gay marriage exposes how capitalism structures our notion of "family" and the privatization of the social relationships we depend on to survive.

In a neoliberal economy, gay identity becomes a way to further capitalist exploitation. In an essay titled "Professional Homosexuals," Katherine Sender writes about gays and lesbians in a high-tech firm trying for years to form a gay and lesbian employee group; such groups were banned for fear they would "function as trade unions." Eventually, the firm allowed such a group to form; it was concerned with the "recruitment ... and productivity of gay and lesbian employees." None of which had to do with them as workers. The point is this: today, capitalism does not seek to exclude gays and lesbians— instead, it seeks to integrate them into its structure of exploitation as long as they don't upset the status quo.

This anthology insists that we stop looking for "equality" in the narrow terms dictated by neoliberalism, where progress means an endless replication of the status quo. It insists that we stop acquiescing to the neoliberal demand that our identities should dictate what basic rights are given to us. *Against Equality* is unapologetic and even, at times, angry. We are not only putting gay marriage advocates on notice, but their "straight allies" as well. In the course of our work over the last many years, we have often been accused by our critics of having no "solutions." Our response, then and now, is that the critique, one that has often been silenced or made invisible, is a necessary part of the process of finding solutions that erase the economic inequality that surrounds us all. Our work is not intended to be prescriptive—unlike marriage, we do not guarantee eternal happiness of the married kind— but to agitate for a much needed dialogue on these matters. Our point, as will be evident from the essays that follow, is that the idea of marriage as any kind of solution for our problems perpetuates the very inequalities that gay marriage advocates claim to resolve.

Against Equality: Who We Are

Against Equality, the collective and website, was begun by Ryan Conrad in November 2009 as an attempt to simply archive a vast array of articles, art, 'zines and other texts that had clearly, over the years, been steadily echoing a strong and growing distrust of and disagreement and disillusionment with the mainstream gay movement. The Against Equality collective is a loose aggregate of people currently located throughout the United States and Canada. The contributors who are a part of this collection may or may not be members of the editorial and/or archival collective.

The collective is comprised of artists, academics, writers, activists and filmmakers (and we are often all of that at the same time). For all of us, the web archive is an unpaid project we participate in because this work is important to us. Our commitment to the archive as a repository of historical work means that we only publish work in its original form, complete with any ideological ghosts that the authors might want to erase from public memory. We have however, allowed a few pieces for the book to be edited, in order to condense longer work or to allow the scope of very specific and localized critiques to resonate more broadly within this new context.

We began the website with a collection of articles on gay marriage, hate crimes legislation and Don't Ask Don't Tell (DADT) that were critical of the politics of the mainstream gay movement. We created a Facebook page soon after, which has by now gained over 1750 members. That is modest by some counts, but our members clearly were and an impassioned bunch. They told us, in message after message, of being tired of the same old rhetoric from the gay marriage movement, of deploring the call to further violence through the prison expansion required by hate crimes legislation and the call to repeal DADT. The Against Equality website is an archive of the ongoing resistance to the assimilationist gay agenda. We do not simply focus on long works by established authors. Rather, we are concerned with gathering in one place the various ephemera, manifestoes, statements, and even graffiti generated by the millions who are weary of being told that to be queer requires them to become perfect neoliberal citizens as well.

After only a few months of archiving, we realized that people's desire to read and share the articles we had brought together was stronger and deeper than anything we had envisioned. We thought it best to begin collecting some of the essays into separate anthologies, each representing one of the subject areas. We wanted to keep the costs low, and to be able to control crucial factors like the cover art and size (we very much wanted it to be literally a pocket-size book, lending itself to the portability of the ideas we were to publish inside). We briefly considered the idea of a 'zine, but decided that while we loved the idea of 'zines (and several of us in the collective are 'zine-makers), we wanted something less ephemeral and more lasting. To that end, we decided to self-publish *Against Equality: Queer Critiques of Gay Marriage*.

We were also concerned about accessibility—not everyone has regular and reliable access to the web, and we know that there are many queers in underserved rural and urban areas for whom such a collection would prove to be a lifeline. As members of a radical, queer movement, we fervently believe that groups engage in acts of resistance by first empowering themselves through the simple act of collectively arguing over and discussing the texts that are vital to them. We could envision such collectivities in real time: groups of people gathered in community centers or the houses of friends as they marked up their copies. We had a much harder time envisioning them gathered around the collective glow emanating from several laptop screens. None of this is to recover a nostalgic and anti-technological framework. Rather, we understand, as a multi-generational and multi-dimensional cohort of people whose forms of activism and writing span a wide range of issues, that the book, in all its bookness, is still the most accessible and dynamic way of gathering people together.

As a self-published project, we could not afford illustrations, but we did want more than word-based texts and to acknowledge that resistance to the mainstream gay movement takes on myriad forms, including art and visual culture. We sent out a call for artwork, and the result is the collection of stunning images that you see in the set of postcards included with the book.

In future, we will be publishing the second and third installments, on hate crimes legislation and DADT. It is our hope that this tiny but potent reminder of our queer past and the mad possibilities of the queer future will make its way around the world in pockets, purses, backpacks, and bags of all sorts.

This piece originally appeared on Kate Bornstein's Blog (katebornstein.typepad.com) on December 4, 2009.

Open Letter to LGBT Leaders Who Are Pushing Marriage Equality

Kate Bornstein

To the leaders, membership, and supporters of The Human Rights Campaign, The National Gay and Lesbian Task Force, and state-wide groups supporting marriage equality as your primary goal,

Hello. I'm Kate Bornstein, and I've got a great deal to say to you, so you deserve to know more about me: I write books about postmodern gender theory and alternatives to suicide for teens, freaks and other outlaws. I'm a feminist, a Taoist, a sadomasochist, a femme, a nerd, a transperson, a Jew, and a tattooed lady. I'm a certified Post Traumatic Stress Disorder survivor. I'm a chronic over-eater who's been diagnosed with anorexia. I'm sober, but I'm not always clean. I've got piercings in body parts I wasn't born with. I'm also an elder in the community you claim to represent, and it is with great sorrow that I must write: you have not been representing us.

Let's talk about a love that unites more people than have ever before been united by love. Let's defend some real equality.

The other day, New York State's lesbian and gay bid for marriage equality went down in flames, enough flames to make people cry. Thousands of lesbians, gay men, bisexuals and transgender people and their allies spent a lot of money and heart-filled hours of work to legalize marriage equality, with little to show for it. That sucks, and I

11

think the reason it didn't work is it's because marriage equality is an incorrect priority for the LGBTQetc communities.

Marriage equality—as it's being pushed for now—is wasting resources that would be better deployed to save some lives. There are several major flaws with marriage equality as a priority for our people:

Marriage as it's practiced in the USA is unconstitutional... if you listen to Thomas Jerfferson's interpretation of separation of church and state. The way it stands now, if you're an ordained leader in a recognized religion, the US government gives you a package of 1500-1700 civil rights that only you can hand out to people. And you get to bestow or withhold these civil rights from any American citizen you choose, regardless of that citizen's constitutionally-granted rights. The government has no constitutional right to hand that judgment call over to a religious body.

Marriage equality—as it's being fought for now by lesbian and gay leaders who claim they're speaking for some majority of LGBTQetc people—will wind up being more marriage inequality. Single parents, many of whom are women of color, will not get the 1500-1700 rights they need to better and more easily raise their children. Nor will many other households made up of any combination of people who love each other and their children.

When lesbian and gay community leaders whip up the community to fight for the right to marry, it's a further expression of America's institutionalized greed in that it benefits only its demographic constituency. There's no reaching out beyond sexuality and gender expression to benefit people who aren't just like us, and honestly... that is so 20th Century identity politics.

Marriage is a privileging institution. It has privileged, and continues to privilege people along lines of not only religion, sexuality and gender, but also along the oppressive vectors of race, class, age, looks, ability, citizenship, family status, and language. Seeking to grab oneself a piece of the marriage-rights pie does little if anything at all for the oppression caused by the institution of marriage itself to many more people than sex and gender outlaws.

The fight for "marriage equality" is simply not the highest priority for a movement based in sexuality and gender. By simple triage, the most widespread criminality against people whose identities are based in sex and gender is violence against women. Women still make up the single-most oppressed identity in the world, followed closely by kids who are determined to be freaky for any reason whatsoever.

Lesbian and gay leaders must cease being self-obsessed and take into account the very real damage that's perpetrated on people who are more than simply lesbian women and/or gay men, more than bisexual or transgender even. Assuming a good-hearted but misplaced motivation for all the work done on behalf of fighting for marriage equality, it's time to stop fighting on that front as a first priority of the LGBTQetc movement. It's time to do some triage and base our priorities on a) who needs the most help and b) what battlefront will bring us the most allies.

I'm asking that you to fight on behalf of change for someone besides yourself. Please. I promise the rewards of doing that will revisit you threefold. Who needs the most help is easy: women. To lesbian and gay leaders, I ask you to ally yourselves with the centuries-old feminist movements and their current incarnations. You want to get a bill passed through Congress? Take another run at the Equal Rights Amendment. Unlike gay marriage, the ERA stands a better chance of making it into law, given the Obama Administration and our loosely Democratic majority in congress.

Stopping the violence against women and freaky children, and backing another run at the ERA have got the good chance of creating national front, lots of allies. On the home front of sex and gender, there's plenty of room for change that doesn't require millions of dollars and thousands of hours.

Looking into the community of people who base their lives on sexuality and gender, there's a lot of door-opening to do. Beyond L, G, B and T, there's also Q for queer and Q for questioning. There's an S for sadomasochists, an I for intersex, an F for feminists, and another F for furries. Our community is additionally composed of sex educators, sex workers, adult entertainers, pornographers, men who have sex with men, women who have sex with women, and asexuals who have sex with no one but themselves. You want to create some real change?

Make room for genderqueers, polyamorists, radical faeries, butches, femmes, drag queens, drag king, and other dragfuck royalty too fabulous to describe in this short letter.

There are more and more people to add to this ever-growing list of communities whom you must own as family and represent in your activism. You cannot afford—politically, economically, or morally—to leave out a single person who bases a large part of their identity on being sex positive or in any way a proponent of gender anarchy.

That's what I have to say to you. That and thank you for the good hearts you've clearly demonstrated in your activism. I'm asking you to open your hearts further is all.

The best way to engage me in a conversation or recruit me to help is to contact me through Twitter. I look forward to talking with you, and I hope we can work together on the terms I've outlined above.

Warmly, and with respect,

Your Auntie Kate

This piece was originally written for a 'zine and action at the Republican National Convention in 2004 entitled "Married to the State: A Shotgun."

Marriage is Murder:
On the Discursive Limits of Matrimony
Eric Stanley

So, what is wrong with gay marriage?

In order to answer that question we must first understand what this thing called marriage is. Marriage is essentially a financial and legal contract that allocates the movement of property, power and privilege from one person to another. Historically it has been a way of consolidating family power amongst and between men, through women. In more recent times marriage in the United States has functioned to solidify the American middle class. Marriage does this through concentrating wealth and power through family lines and inheritance (both in terms of money and power). Because of marriage's ability to discipline class structures it is now, and always has been, a primary structure of a capitalist economy. In reality most people marry within their own socioeconomic class.

Marriage, earlier through miscegenation laws, and currently through racist "values," also contains wealth through racist ideologies of matrimony. Because of these realities there has been a long history of critique of the institution of marriage launched by feminists of color, white feminists, and queer people among others.

What about gay marriage? Isn't gay marriage going to change all of this?

NO. The current push towards gay marriage is, in fact, not going to subvert the systems of domination we all live through. Ironically, the gay marriage movement is standing on these same legacies of brutality for their slice of the wedding cake. Take for example the "Freedom to Marry" stickers created by the Freedom to Marry organization. Not only are these stickers falsely equating the intervention of the State into one's life (marriage) with "freedom" (when was the last time the State helped you to become more "free"?) they are trying to work this idea through horrifying star-spangled stickers. Instead of critiquing the ways US imperialism has rendered most transgender people, queer people, people or color etc. as expendable through its countless wars here and abroad, the Freedom To Marry stickers simply disguise these histories and reproduce this red-white-and-blue national theme for every married gay and guilt-filled liberal to wear with PRIDE.

If straight people can marry, why should gay people not have the same privilege?

What we are calling for is an abolishment of State sanctioned coupling in either the hetero or homo incarnation. We are against any institution that perpetuates the further exploitation of some people for the benefit of others. Why do the fundamental necessities marriage may provide for some (like healthcare) have to be wedded to the State sanctioned ritual of terror known as marriage?

Won`t gay marriage help couples stay together where one person is not a US citizen?

The way immigration is being used by the gay marriage movement is not only un-thought-out but also relies on racist notions of the "white man saving his brown lover". Although it is true that because of the US policies on immigration some lesbian and gay couples may be split, gay marriage does not at all question these systems that allow some people into the country (white) while excluding others (people of color). Where are the gay marriage "activists" when the INS is actively raiding and deporting whole families? (such as it is currently doing just blocks away from the Castro in San Francisco's Mission District). Also missing from the picture of immigration that gay marriage advocates are painting is the reality that there are queer couples in the US where

16

neither person is a US citizen. How will gay marriage help them stay in the US if that is what they want to do? Gay marriage will not challenge "citizenship" but simply place some bodies within its grasp while holding others out.

I agree with your argument, but isn't gay marriage a step in the right direction?

This liberal model of "progression" is one of the primary ways many of us are ideologically trapped into a reformist way of thinking. To understand how gay marriage, like voting, will never lead to liberation we can look to the histories of many "social justice movements" that only address oppressions on a level of the symptomatic. Gay marriage and voting are symbolic gestures that reinforce structures while claiming to reconfigure them. This scheme will undoubtedly become apparent with "marriage equality" advocates. As they have positioned gay marriage as the last great civil rights battle, will they continue to fight after the Honeymoon?

Won't gay marriage help get health care to more people?

It may help some people get healthcare but for the vast majority of Americans with NO healthcare it will do nothing. And within the rhetoric of the gay marriage movement, working towards healthcare for all (people and animals) is nowhere to be found. This argument also relies on the false assumption that one person would already have healthcare.

So if you are against gay marriage then you are allying with the Christian Right and the GOP!

NO. This is amongst the most troubling aspects of this current epidemic of gay marriage. The way the marriage movement is framing any critique of their precious institution is either you are one of us (gay married) or you are one of them (homophobe). This helps to silence the much needed debate and public discourse around such issues. It seems as if everyone has been shamed into submission and subsequent silence by the marriage movement. Even in allegedly "progressive" circles any mention of the implicit links between marriage, misogyny, and racism in the U.S. gets shut down by a "gay married".

Ironically, if you look at the rhetoric of the Freedom to Marry movement and the Republican Party, their similarities are frighteningly apparent. In their ideal world we would all be monogamously coupled, instead of rethinking the practice of "coupling." They want us working our jobs, not working towards collective and self-determination, remembering anniversaries not the murder of trans-people, buying wedding rings not smashing capitalism. The vision of the future the Republicans and the gay marriage movement have offered will render most of us already in the margins of the picture (trans-people, sex workers, queers of color, HIV positive people, non-monogamous people etc.) as the new enemy of the régime of married normalcy they hope to usher in.

This statement was originally published on facebook in 2008 and was then circulated online via makezine.enoughenough.org.

I Still Think Marriage is the Wrong Goal

Dean Spade and Crag Willse

A lot of stories are circulating right now claiming that Black and Latino voters are to blame for Prop 8 passing. Beneath this claim is an un-interrogated idea that people of color are "more homophobic" than white people. Such an idea equates gayness with whiteness and erases the lives of LGBT people of color. It also erases and marginalizes the enduring radical work of LGBT people of color organizing that has prioritized the most vulnerable members of our communities.

Current conversations about Prop 8 hide how the same-sex marriage battle has been part of a conservative gay politics that de-prioritizes people of color, poor people, trans people, women, immigrants, prisoners and people with disabilities. Why isn't Prop 8's passage framed as evidence of the mainstream gay agenda's failure to ally with people of color on issues that are central to racial and economic justice in the US?

Let's remember the politics of marriage itself. The simplistic formula that claims "you're either pro-marriage or against equality" makes us forget that all forms of marriage perpetuate gender, racial and economic inequality. It mistakenly assumes that support for marriage is the only good measure of support for LGBT communities. This political moment calls for anti-homophobic politics that centralize anti-racism and anti-poverty. Marriage is a coercive state structure that perpetuates racism and sexism through forced gender and family norms. Right wing pro-marriage rhetoric has targeted families of color and poor families, supported a violent welfare and child protection system, vilified single parents and women, and marginalized queer families of all kinds. Expanding marriage to include a narrow band of same-sex couples only strengthens that system of marginalization and supports the idea that the state should pick which types of families to reward and recognize and which to punish and endanger.

We still demand a queer political agenda that centralizes the experiences of prisoners, poor people, immigrants, trans people, and people with disabilities. We reject a gay agenda that pours millions of dollars into campaigns for access to oppressive institutions for a few that stand to benefit.

We are being told marriage is the way to solve gay people's problems with health care access, immigration, child custody, and symbolic equality. It does not solve these problems, and there are real campaigns and struggles that would and could approach these problems for everyone, not just for a privileged few. Let's take the energy and money being put into gay marriage and put it toward real change: opposing the War on Terror and all forms of endless war; supporting queer prisoners and building a movement to end imprisonment; organizing against police profiling and brutality in our communities; fighting attacks on welfare, public housing and Medicaid; fighting for universal health care that is trans and reproductive healthcare inclusive; fighting to tax wealth not workers; fighting for a world in which no one is illegal.

This piece was originally published on March 5, 2004 and has been re-posted on numerous websites.

Is Gay Marriage Anti Black???

Kenyon Farrow

I was in Atlanta on business when I saw the Sunday, Feb. 29th edition of the *Atlanta Journal Constitution* that featured as its cover story the issue of gay marriage. Georgia is one of the states prepared to add some additional language to its state constitution that bans same sex marriages (though the state already defines marriage between a man and a woman, so the legislation is completely symbolic as it is political).

What struck me about the front-page story was the fact that all of the average Atlanta citizens who were pictured that opposed gay marriages were black people. This is not to single out the *Atlanta Journal Constitution*, as I have noticed in all of the recent coverage and hubbub over gay marriage that the media has been really crucial in playing up the racial politics of the debate.

For example, the people who are in San Francisco getting married are almost exclusively white whereas many of the people who are shown opposing it are black. And it is more black people than typically shown in the evening news (not in handcuffs). This leaves me with several questions: Is gay marriage a black/white issue? Are the Gay Community and the Black Community natural allies or sworn enemies?

And where does that leave me, a black gay man, who does not want to get married?

Same-sex Marriage and Race Politics

My sister really believes that this push for gay marriage is actually not being controlled by gays & lesbians. She believes it is actually being tested in various states by the Far Right in disguise, in an effort to cause major fractures in the Democratic Party to distract from all the possible roadblocks to re-election for George W. in November such as an unpopular war and occupation, the continued loss of jobs, and growing revelations of the Bush administration's ties to corporate scandals.

Whatever the case, it is important to remember that gay marriage rights are fraught with racial politics, and that there is no question that the public opposition to same-sex marriages is in large part being financially backed by various right-wing Christian groups like the Christian Coalition and Family Research Council. Both groups have histories and overlapping staff ties to white supremacist groups and solidly oppose affirmative action but play up some sort of Christian allegiance to the black Community when the gay marriage issue is involved.

For example, in the 1990s the Traditional Values Coalition produced a short documentary called "Gay Rights, Special Rights," which was targeted at black churches to paint non-heterosexual people as only white and upper class, and as sexual pariahs, while painting black people as pure, chaste, and morally superior.

The video juxtaposed images of white gay men for the leather/S&M community with the voice of Dr. Martin Luther King's "I Have a Dream" speech, leaving conservative black viewers with the fear that the Civil Rights Movement was being taken over by morally debased human beings. And since black people continue to be represented as hyper-sexual beings and sexual predators in both pop culture and the mass media as pimps & players, hoochies & hos, rapists of white women & tempters of white men, conservative black people often cling to the other image white America hoists onto black people as well—asexual and morally superior (as seen in the role of the black talk show host and the role of the black sage/savior-of-white people used in so many Hollywood movies, like *In America* and *The Green Mile*, which are all traceable to Mammy and Uncle Remus-type caricatures).

Since the Christian Right has money and access to corporate media, they set the racial/sexual paradigm that much of America gets in this debate, which is that homos are rich and white and do not need any such special protections and that black people are black—a homogeneous group who, in this case, are Christian, asexual (or hetero-normative), morally superior, and have the right type of "family values." This, even though black families are consistently painted as dysfunctional and are treated as such in the mass media and in public policy, which has devastating effects on black self-esteem, and urban and rural black communities' ability to be self-supporting, self-sustaining, and self determining.

The lack of control over economic resources, high un/underemployment, lack of adequate funding for targeted effective HIV prevention and treatment, and the large numbers of black people in prison (nearly one million of the 2.2 million U.S. prison population) are all ways that black families (which include non-heterosexuals) are undermined by public policies often fueled by right wing "tough on crime" and "war on drugs" rhetoric.

Given all of these social problems that largely plague the black community (and thinking about my sister's theory), one has to wonder why this issue would rise to the surface in an election year, just when the Democratic ticket is unifying. And it is an issue, according to the polls anyway, that could potentially strip the Democratic Party of its solid support from African-American communities.

And even though several old-guard civil rights leaders (including Coretta Scott King, John Lewis, Revs. Al Sharpton, and Jesse Jackson) have long supported equal protection under the law for the gay, lesbian, bisexual and transgender community (which usually, but not always means support of same-sex marriage), the right wing continues to pit gay marriage (and by extension, gay civil rights) against black political interests, by relying on conservative black people to publicly speak out against it (and a lot has been written about how several black ministers received monies from right-wing organizations to speak out against same-sex marriages in their pulpits).

But many black leaders, including some I've been able to catch on television recently despite the right-wing's spin on the matter, have made the argument that they know too well the dangers that lie in "separate but equal" rhetoric. So, if many of our black leaders vocally support same-sex marriage, how has the Christian Right been able to create such a wedge between the black community and the gay community?

Homophobia in Black Popular Culture

Some of the ways that the Christian Right-wing has been so successful in using same-sex marriage as a wedge issue is by both exploiting homophobia in the black community and also racism in the gay community. In regards to homophobia in the black community the focus of conversation has been about the Black Churches' stance on homosexuality.

It has been said many times that while many black churches remain somewhat hostile places for non-heterosexual parishioners, it is also where you will in fact find many black gays and lesbians. Many of them are in positions of power and leadership within the church—ushers, choir members/directors, musicians, and even preachers themselves.

But let me debunk the myth that the Black Church is the black community. The black community is in no way monolithic, nor are black Christians. The vast majority of black people who identify as "Christian" do not attend any church whatsoever. Many black Americans have been Muslim for over a century and there are larger numbers of black people who are proudly identifying as Yoruba, Santero/a, and atheists as well.

The black community in America is also growing more ethnically diverse, with a larger, more visible presence of Africans, West Indians, and Afro-Latinos amongst our ranks. We have always been politically diverse, with conservatives, liberals, radicals and revolutionaries alike (and politics do not necessarily align with what religion you may identify as your own). It is also true that we are and have always been sexually diverse and multi-gendered. Many of our well-known Black History Month favorites were in fact Gay, Bisexual, Lesbian, or Transgender.

Despite our internal diversity, we are at a time (for the last 30 years) when black people are portrayed in the mass media—mostly through hip-hop culture—as being hyper-sexual and *hyper-heterosexual* to be specific. Nowhere is the performance of black masculinity more prevalent than in hip-hop culture, which is where the most palpable form of homophobia in American culture currently resides.

This of course is due largely to the white record industry's notions of who we are, which they also sell to non-black people. Remember pop culture has for the last 150 years been presenting blackness to the world—initially as white performers in blackface, to black performers in blackface, and currently to white, black and other racial groups performing blackness as something that connotes sexual potency and a propensity for violent behavior, which are also performed as heterosexuality.

And with the music video, performance is important (if not more) than song content. As black hip-hop artists perform gangsta and Black Nationalist revolutionary forms of masculinity alike, so follows overt homophobia and hostility to queer people, gay men in particular. Recently, DMX's video and song "Where the Hood At?" contained some of the most blatant and hateful homophobic lyrics and images I have seen in about a decade.

The song suggests that the "faggot" can and will never be part of the "hood" for he is not a man. The song and video are particularly targeted at black men who are not out of the closet, and considered on the "down low." Although challenged by DMX, the image of the "down low" brother is another form of performance of black masculinity, regardless of actual sexual preference.

But it's not just "commercial" rap artists being homophobic. "Conscious" hip–hop artists such as Common, Dead Prez and Mos Def have also promoted homophobia through their lyrics, mostly around notions of "strong black families," and since gay black men (in theory) do not have children, we are somehow anti-family and antithetical to what a "strong black man" should be.

Lesbians (who are not interested in performing sex acts for the pleasure of male voyeurs) are also seen as anti-family, and not a part of the black community. A woman "not wanting dick" in a nation where black dick is the only tangible power symbol for black men is seen as just plain crazy, which is also expressed in many hip-hop tunes. None of these artists interrogate their representations of masculinity in their music, but merely perform them for street credibility. And for white market consumption.

It cannot be taken lightly that white men are in control of the record industry as a whole (even with a few black entrepreneurs), and control what images get played. Young white suburban males are the largest consumers of hip-hop music. So performance of black masculinity (or black sexuality as a whole) is created by white men for white men. And since white men have always portrayed black men as sexually dangerous and black women as always sexually available (and sexual violence against black women is rarely taken seriously), simplistic representations of black sexuality as hyper-heterosexual are important to maintaining white supremacy and patriarchy, and control of black bodies.

Black people are merely the unfortunate middlemen in an exchange between white men. We consume the representations like the rest of America. And the more that black people are willing to accept these representations as fact rather than racist fiction, the more heightened homophobia in our communities tends to be.

Race and the Gay Community

While homophobia in the black community is certainly an issue we need to address, blacks of all sexualities experience the reality that many white gays and lesbians think that because they're gay, they "understand" oppression, and therefore could not be racist like their heterosexual counterparts. Bullshit.

America is first built on the privilege of whiteness, and as long as you have white skin, you have a level of agency and access above and beyond people of color, period. White women and white non-heteros included. There is a white gay man named Charles Knipp who roams this nation performing drag in blackface to sold-out houses, north and south alike. Just this past Valentine's day weekend, he performed at the Slide Bar in NY's east village to a packed house of white queer folks eager to see him perform "Shirley Q Liquor," a welfare mother with 19 kids.

And haven't all of the popular culture gay images on TV shows like *Will & Grace*, *Queer as Folk*, etc., been exclusively white? No matter how many black divas wail over club beats in white gay clubs all over America (Mammy goes disco!) with gay men appropriating language and other black cultural norms (specifically from black women), white gay men continue to function as cultural imperialists the same way straight white boys appropriate hip-hop (and let's not ignore that white women have been in on the act, largely a result of Madonna bringing white women into the game).

There have always been racial tensions in the gay community as long as there have been racial tensions in America, but in the 1990s, the white gay community went mainstream, further pushing non-hetero people of color from the movement.

The reason for this schism is that in order to be mainstream in America, one has to be seen as white. And since white is normative, one has to interrogate what other labels or institutions are seen as normative in our society: family, marriage, and military service, to name a few. It is then no surprise that a movement that goes for "normality" would then end up in a battle over a dubious institution like marriage (and hetero-normative family structures by extension).

And debates over "family values," no matter how broad or narrow you look at them, always have whiteness at the center, and are almost always anti-black. As articulated by Robin D.G. Kelley in his book *Yo Mama's Dysfunktional*, the infamous Moynihan report is the most egregious of examples of how the black family structure has been portrayed as dysfunctional, an image that still has influence on the way in which black families are discussed in the media and controlled by law enforcement and public policy.

Since black families are in fact presented and treated as dysfunctional, this explains the large numbers of black children in the hands of the state through foster care, and increasingly, prisons (so-called "youth detention centers"). In many cases, trans-racial adoptions are the result. Many white same-sex unions take advantage of the state's treatment of black families; after all, white queer couples are known for adopting black children since they are so "readily" available and also not considered as attractive or healthy compared to white, Asian and Latino/a kids.

If black families were not labeled as dysfunctional or de-stabilized by prison expansion and welfare "reform," our children would not be removed from their homes at the numbers they are, and there would be no need for adoption or foster care in the first place. So the fact that the white gay community continues to use white images of same-sex families is no accident, since the black family, heterosexual, same sex or otherwise, is always portrayed as dysfunctional.

I also think the white gay community's supposed "understanding" of racism is what has caused them to appropriate the language and ideology of the Black Civil Rights Movement, which has led to the bitter divide between the two communities. This is where I, as a black gay man, am forced to intervene in a debate that I find problematic on all sides.

Black Community and Gay Community—Natural Allies or Sworn Enemies?

As the gay community moved more to the right in the 1990s, they also began to talk about Gay Rights as Civil Rights. Even today in this gay marriage debate, I have heard countless well-groomed, well-fed white gays and lesbians on TV referring to themselves as "second-class citizens." Jason West, the white mayor of New Paltz, NY, who started marrying gay couples was quoted as saying, "The same people who don't want to see gays and lesbians get married are the same people who would have made Rosa Parks go to the back of the bus."

It's these comparisons that piss black people off. While the anger of black heteros is sometimes expressed in ways that are in fact homophobic, the truth of the matter is that black folks are tired of seeing other people hijack their shit for their own gains, and getting nothing in return. Black non-heteros share this anger of having our blackness and black political rhetoric and struggle stolen for other people's gains.

The hijacking of Rosa Parks for their campaigns clearly ignores the fact that white gays and lesbians who lived in Montgomery, AL and elsewhere probably gladly made many a black person go to the back of the bus. James Baldwin wrote in his long essay "No Name in the Street" about how he was felt up by a white sheriff in a small southern town when on a visit during the civil rights era.

These comparisons of "Gay Civil Rights" as equal to "Black Civil Rights" really began in the early 1990s, and largely responsible for this was the Human Rights Campaign (HRC) and a few other mostly-white gay organizations. This push from the HRC, without any visible black leadership or tangible support from black allies (straight and queer), to equate these movements did several things: 1) Pissed off the black community for the white gay movement's cultural appropriation, and made the straight black community question non-hetero black people's allegiances, resulting in our further isolation. 2) Gave the (white) Christian Right ammunition to build relationships with black ministers to denounce gay rights from their pulpits based on the HRC's cultural appropriation. 3) Created a scenario in their effort to go mainstream that equated gay and lesbian with upper-class and white.

This meant that the only visibility of non-hetero poor people and people of color wound up on *Jerry Springer*, where non-heteros who are poor and of color are encouraged (and paid) to act out, and are therefore only represented as dishonest, violent, and pathological.

So, given this difficult history and problematic working relationship of the black community and the gay community, how can the gay community now, at its most crucial hour, expect large scale support of same-sex marriage by the black community when there has been no real work done to build strategic allies with us? A new coalition has formed of black people, non-hetero and hetero, to promote same-sex marriage equality to the black community, and I assume to effectively bridge that disconnect, and to in effect say that gay marriage ain't just a white thing. Or is it?

Is Gay Marriage Anti–Black?

I, as a black gay man, do not support this push for same-sex marriage. Although I don't claim to represent all black gay people, I do believe that the manner in which this campaign has been handled has put black people in the middle of essentially two white groups of people, who are trying to manipulate us one way or the other. The Christian Right, which is in fact anti-black, has tried to create a false alliance between themselves and blacks through religion to push forward their homophobic, fascist agenda.

The white gay civil rights groups are also anti-black, however they want black people to see this struggle for same-sex unions as tantamount to separate but equal Jim Crow laws. Yet any close examination reveals that histories of terror imposed upon generations of all black people in this country do not in any way compare to what appears to be the very last barrier between white gays and lesbians' access to what bell hooks describes as "christian capitalist patriarchy."

That system is inherently anti-black, and no amount of civil rights will ever get black people any real liberation from it. For, in what is now a good 40 years of "civil rights," nothing has intrinsically changed or altered in the American power structure, and a few black faces in inherently racist institutions is hardly progress.

Given the current white hetero-normative constructions of family and how the institutions of marriage and nuclear families have been used against black people, I do think that to support same-sex marriage is in fact, anti-black (I also believe the institution of marriage to be historically anti-woman, and don't support it for those reasons as well).

At this point I don't know if I am totally opposed to the institution of marriage altogether, but I do know that the campaign would have to happen on very different terms for me to support same-sex marriages. At this point, the white gay community is as much to blame as the Christian Right for the way they have constructed the campaign, including who is represented, and their appropriation of black civil rights language.

Along with how the campaign is currently devised, I struggle with same-sex marriage because, given the level of homophobia in our society (specifically in the black community), and racism as well, I think that even if same-sex marriage becomes legal, white people will access that privilege far more than black people. This is especially the case with poor black people who, regardless of sexual preference or gender, are struggling with the most critical of needs (housing, food, gainful employment), which are not at all met by same-sex marriage.

Some black people (men in particular) might not try to access same-sex marriage because they do not even identify as "gay" partly because of homophobia in the black community, but also because of the fact that racist white queer people continue to dominate the public discourse of what "gay" is, which does not include black people of the hip-hop generation by and large.

I do fully understand that non-heteros of all races and classes may cheer this effort for they want their love to be recognized, and may want to reap some of the practical benefits that a marriage entitlement would bring—health care (if one of you gets health care from your job in the first place) for your spouse, hospital visits without drama or scrutiny, and control over a deceased partner's estate.

But, gay marriage, in and of itself, is not a move towards real and systemic liberation. It does not address my most critical need as a black gay man to be able to walk down the streets of my community with my lover, spouse or trick, and not be subjected to ridicule, assault, or even murder. Gay marriage does not adequately address homophobia or transphobia, for same-sex marriage still implies binary opposite thinking, and transgender folks are not at all addressed in this debate.

What does gay marriage mean for all Black people?

But what does that mean for black people? For black non-heteros, specifically? Am I supposed to get behind this effort, and convince heterosexual black people to do the same, especially when I know the racist manner in which this campaign has been carried out for over ten years? And especially when I know that the vast majority of issues that my community—The Black Community, of all orientations and genders—are not taken nearly this seriously when it comes to crucial life and death issues that we face daily like inadequate housing and health care, HIV/AIDS, police brutality, and the wholesale lockdown of an entire generation in America's grotesquely large prison system.

How do those of us who are non-heterosexual and black use this as an opportunity to deal with homophobia, transphobia and misogyny in our communities, and heal those larger wounds of isolation, marginalization and fear that plague us regardless of marital status? It is the undoing of systems of domination and control that will lead to liberation for all of ourselves, and all of us as a whole.

In the end, I am down for black people who oppose gay marriage— other folks "in the life" as well as straight, feminists, Christians, Muslims, and the like. But I want more than just quotes from Leviticus or other religious and moral posturing. I want to engage in a meaningful critical conversation of what this means for *all* of us, which means that I must not be afraid to *be* me in our community, and you must not be afraid *of* me. I will struggle alongside you, but I must know that you will also have my back.

This piece, which includes a reprint of another text by the same authors from 1996, originally appeared in the April 2004 issue of UltraViolet.

Marriage Is Still the Opiate of the Queers
Kate and Deeg

"We want the abolition of the institution of the bourgeois nuclear family. We believe that the bourgeois nuclear family perpetuates the false categories of homosexuality and heterosexuality by creating sex roles, sex definitions and sexual exploitation. The bourgeois nuclear family as the basic unit of capitalism creates oppressive roles of homosexuality and heterosexuality... It is every child's right to develop in a non-sexist, non-racist, non-possessive atmosphere which is the responsibility of all people, including gays, to create."

— "Third World Gay Liberation Manifesto," New York City (circa 1970)

"The struggle for civil rights within the context of this society can, at best, result in second class status and toleration by a wretched straight society. The struggle for democratic or civil rights assumes that the system is basically okay, and that its flaws can be corrected through legal reform....We demand the right of all lesbians and gay men, and children to live in the manner we choose."

— "Gay Liberation, Not Just Gay Rights!" LAGAI, Lavender Left (Los Angeles) and Lesbian and Gay Liberation and Solidarity Committee (New York), 1987

*   *   *

A specter is haunting Amerikkka.

The specter of gay marriage.

Every few years, it seems, we have a new wave of push and counterpush on the marriage issue, and we are always in the same unpleasant position. We demand all civil rights for queer people.

But marriage isn't a civil right. It's a civil wrong.

Just because George W., Pete KKKnight and the KKKristian RRRight don't want us to get married, doesn't mean we have to want to.

In 1996, we held our legendary First Ever Mass Gay Divorce on Castro Street, where a good time was had by all at the dish breaking booth and the Go Your Separate Ways Travel Agency. At that time, we wrote the following flier:

"Remember us? We are lesbians and gay men, the people who choose love, and sex, over societal acceptance, over physical security, over the almighty buck.

We pursue our love into the cities and towns where we find each other. What a wonderful variety of relationships we have - from anonymous or casual sex in baths, bathrooms and beaches, to long-term monogamy and everything (and everyone) in between. We say, "the state can't tell us who, or how, to love." We say, "Get your laws off my body." So how exactly does that become a plea to the state to marry us? Will having state-defined relationships make us better lovers? It hasn't done much for hets.

We always thought that one of the good things about being a lesbian, or gay man, is that you don't have to get married. Many of us have parents who are or were married, and really, it's nothing to write home about.

The heterosexual nuclear family is the most dangerous place to be. A woman is beaten every 15 seconds. One girl in three is sexually molested by the time she reaches maturity. According to the National Coalition to Prevent Child Abuse, one million children were abused last year, and 1,000 were killed. 46 percent of the murdered children were not yet one year old.

We're here today because we were lucky enough to survive these odds.

When our gay leaders talk about how gay marriage will support the institution of marriage in this society, we have to agree. We would oppose it for this reason alone.

It is interesting that while assimilationists clamor for gay marriage, the right wing is trying to hold straight marriages together by eliminating no-fault divorce. Strange bedfellows?

Gay marriage might give some married gay people access to health care, tax breaks, and immigration rights. But shouldn't our community be fighting for us all to have access to health care, whatever our "marital status?" The same for immigration. Somehow, in these right-wing times, money, goods, and jobs are free to flow across the border, but not people. Shouldn't everyone be able to live where they want to, who made these borders anyhow? And why should any married people pay less taxes? What assimilationist gays are really asking is that the heterosexuals share some of their privilege with queers who want to be like them.

There is a basic conflict here, between those who see the gay movement as a way to gain acceptance in straight society, and lesbians and gay men who are fighting to create a society in our own image. A decent and humane society where we can be free. We do not want the crumbs from this society's table, and we are not fighting for a place at it. We want to overturn the fucking table.

Assimilation is NOT liberation"

We couldn't have said it better. Oh, yeah, we did say it.

The origins of the LGBTQ movement are revolutionary. The rebellions at Stonewall and San Francisco City Hall were led by drag queens and butches who rejected heterosexual roles and restrictions, who were inspired by the revolutionary example of the Black Panthers and the Women's International Terrorist Conspiracy from Hell (WITCH). Now, some of the same people who participated in those fabulous outpourings of anti-establishment rage tripped over each other on the way to City Hall to have their love blessed by Gavin Newsom, successor to Dan White and Dianne Feinstein, darling of the developers, persecutor of the homeless, and the cause of Gay Shame getting beaten and busted by the cops on more than one occasion.

For many older lesbian and gay couples, who recall the days when they could not go to a bar without fear, the chance for official sanction of their love feels like a chance for acceptance after a lifetime of oppression. We respect their choice. But we continue to demand that we honor all our relationships, not just the ones that mimic straight capitalist society.

We remind queer people everywhere that we did not survive the early days of the AIDS epidemic because of the relationships between one man and one man, but because of the strong love of our communities: the health care teams of gay men, lesbians, fag hags and chosen families who spent days and weeks hanging around the intensive care units of Kaiser and Pacific Presbyterian Medical Center, refusing to leave when told "family only," fighting bitterly with biological family members who showed up trying to cram their loved ones into a box and whisk them back to Iowa or New Jersey to be buried with crosses or tallises.

According to a 2004 General Accounting Office report, there are 1,138 federal rights and responsibilities that are automatically accorded to married people. Why should we fight for 1,138 rights for some people, instead of all rights for all people? If Freedom To Marry and the Human Rights Campaign Fund (of course, what can you expect from the folks who brought you the equals sign?) put the resources they have already spent on the "right" to get married into fighting for health coverage for all residents of this rich country (not "virtually all Americans" as "promised" by future president John Kerry) and housing for all the queer youth kicked out by their families and living on the streets, we would have a much better world by now.

Every so-called communist organization in town is suddenly joining the battle cry for marriage. Huh? Have they forgotten their Engels? It is testimony to the fundamental homophobia of the left that they are only comfortable fighting for the most puritan of queer rights. Where were they when the bathhouses were being closed? The left has never recognized queer liberation as the truly revolutionary movement that it is. It is time they did.

The right-wingers say marriage is a sacred religious institution. We agree. The state has no business getting involved in religious institutions, from sanctioning personal unions to legislating what schoolgirls should wear on their heads.

Of course, we too will be fighting to defeat the anti-queer marriage amendments. How can we not? But we resent having to do it, and we will not allow it to distract us from our real needs: equality, justice, self-determination and self-actualization for ALL. Just because you are not someone's significant other, does not mean you are insignificant.

This piece originally appeared in the November-December 2006 issue of The Gay and Lesbian Review

The Marriage Fight is Setting Us Back
John D'Emilio

Even before the morning paper was delivered to my door, I had a long string of e-mails from news groups and organizations announcing the decision in the New York same-sex marriage case. Once again, a major defeat. Over the next weeks, a few more piled up. In the last dozen years, in almost every one of the fifty states, overwhelming majorities in state legislatures or lopsided votes in ballot referenda have reaffirmed that marriage is the union of a man and a woman.

Even the few victories for seekers of the right to marry have morphed into defeats. Legislators and voters undid favorable court opinions in Hawaii and Alaska. And, thanks to the insistence of marriage activists that only the real thing will do, the enactment of civil unions in Vermont and Connecticut and marriage-type rights in California and New Jersey have come to seem like a consolation prize, a spruced-up version of inferiority.

Please, can we speak the truth? The campaign for same-sex marriage has been an unmitigated disaster. Never in the history of organized queerdom have we seen defeats of this magnitude. The battle to win marriage equality through the courts has done something that no other campaign or issue in our movement has done: it has created a vast body of *new* antigay law. Alas for us, as the anthropologist Gayle Rubin has so cogently observed, "sex laws are notoriously easy to pass. ... Once they are on the books, they are extremely difficult to dislodge. "

While outrage and shock over judicial defeats make for good quotes in the press, this disaster should surprise only those activists and ideologues who are utterly convinced of their own rectitude and wisdom. Their determination to get marriage has blinded them to the glaring flaws in the strategy of making marriage equality the prime goal of the gay and lesbian movement, and litigation the main way to achieve it. For one thing, the federal courts and many state courts have grown steadily more conservative for a generation. Did any one really believe that the courts in this era would lead the way on marriage equality?

Then, too, our ever more right-of-center Supreme Court, to which this issue must finally come, has not generally led in struggles for social justice. Rather, it has tended to intervene as a new social consensus develops. Decisions like *Brown v. Board of Education* and *Roe v. Wade* do not prove that social movements should turn to the courts to deliver justice. Instead they show that litigation produces the desired results only after a lot of groundwork outside the courts has been laid. What groundwork for same-sex marriage had been laid when the first cases went forward in the 1990s? What groundwork had been laid for the more recent cases that marriage activists pushed forward *after* countless legislatures and hordes of voters reaffirmed that marriage is the union of a man and a woman?

But putting aside the tactical stupidity of the marriage activist, if there's a single overarching reason why their determined focus on same-sex marriage has disturbed me, it is this: in the deepest, most profound sense, the campaign for marriage equality runs *against history*.

The last half-century has seen one of the most remarkable social transformations in U.S. history. A group of people despised by virtually everyone, hounded and pursued by government officials and law enforcement agents, condemned by every significant religious tradition, and pathologized by scientific experts now has taken its place among the panoply of groups — ethnic, racial, religious—that claim recognition and legitimacy in public life. A group of people who, five decades ago, went to great lengths to mask their sexual identity from anyone who didn't share it now goes to great lengths to display it in every possible venue—at family gatherings and alumni reunions, in occupational associations and workplaces, at school and in places of worship, in massive parades and international athletic competitions. This is quite extraordinary.

How did this happen? As someone who has researched, written about, and participated in our political movement for more than thirty years, I have a bias toward attributing the change to the power of organized collective activism. Lots of individuals saying "this is intolerable and has to change" and then banding together to do something about it has been vital.

AIDS, too, has had something to do with it. Within a few concentrated years it drove out of the closet huge numbers of us, who in turn built a vast network of organizations, engaged with a broad range of institutions, and made demands of public officials. AIDS proved a much more effective mobilizer of people than either the call of sexual freedom or the lure of smashing patriarchy.

But when I put my activist bias aside, the only way to really understand the remarkable transformation in queer life since the 1950s is to move beyond specific events, campaigns, and motivators—beyond Stonewall, Anita Bryant, AIDS. Instead, I have to acknowledge that over the last half-century we have been carried along in the wake of some deep and broad transformations in the patterns of everyday life in the U.S. Think, for a minute, of 1950s television: *Father Knows Best*, *Leave It to Beaver*, *The Donna Reed Show*—all those happy white families, living in nice houses, with mom tending the home and dad at work. Pregnancy out of marriage was a scandal to be hidden away. Divorce was a shameful failure. Childlessness was a pitiable tragedy. In this environment, faggots and dykes were beyond the pale, regarded as deviant and dangerous.

Starting in the 1960s, all this began to change. Divorce became increasingly commonplace. Even with greater access to abortion, large numbers of women had children outside of marriage. The number of single-parent households grew. Cohabitation of unmarried men and women became so widespread that the Bureau of the Census began to categorize and count the phenomenon. Women's participation in the paid labor force skyrocketed. Birth rates sank to replacement levels. The living arrangements of heterosexual Americans became bewilderingly varied. Over the course of a lifetime an individual might move in with a partner, break up with that partner and find another, get married, have a child, get divorced, cohabit with someone else who also had a child (or didn't), break up again, cohabit again, marry again, and become a stepparent. Throughout this saga, all the adults involved were working for a living.

A succinct way of describing these changes is this: *Since the early 1960s, the lives of many, many heterosexuals have become much more like the imagined lives of homosexuals.* Being heterosexual no longer means settling as a young adult into a lifelong coupled relationship sanctioned by the state and characterized by the presence of children and sharply gendered spousal roles. Instead, there may be a number of intimate relationships over the course of a lifetime. A marriage certificate may or may not accompany these relationships. Males and females alike expect to earn their way. Children figure less importantly in the lifespan of adults, and some heterosexuals, for the first time in history, choose not to have children at all.

These changes are not aberrational, not temporary, and not reversible. Neither a decline in morality nor the cultural turbulence of the 1960s explains them. They were not caused by a media culture that exploits sex. Instead, these changes are joined at the hip with the revolutionary growth in economic productivity and technological innovation to which capitalism has given rise and that now have their own momentum. These new "lifestyles" (a word woefully inadequate for grasping the deep structural foundations that sustain these changes) have appeared wherever capitalism has long historical roots. The decline in reproductive rates and the de-centering of marriage follow the spread of capitalism as surely as night follows day. They surface even in the face of religious traditions and national histories that have emphasized marriage, high fertility, and strong kinship ties.

If you need more evidence that the new shape of social life is not a passing heterosexual phase, look at the pathetic failure of efforts to reverse these trends. Since the mid-1970s, the most dynamic and aggressive force in American politics has been the evangelical Christian Right. It has the numbers, the money, the organization, the passion. It can send people into voting booths like no other group in the U.S. Evangelical conservatives have made issues of family and sexual morality the centerpiece of their message and their mobilizations. Because of them, abortions are harder to get, an abstinence-only message dominates sex education, and pre-marital counseling has become the rage. Yet the birth rate remains low, the young are still having sex and cohabiting, and divorce is commonplace.

Grasping the revolutionary change in the lives of heterosexuals in the last half-century lets us put a whole different spin on the transformation in the status of gays and lesbians in the U.S. in the same time period. The huge steps toward visibility, toward acceptance, toward integration, toward equality —and they have been huge—have come, fundamentally, because the life course of heterosexuals has become more like ours. We've made gains not because we've shown heterosexuals that we are just like them, or because we've persuaded them to respect our "differences," but because many of them have become so much like us that they find us less threatening, less dangerous, less strange. In other words, for the last several decades, our lives have been flowing with the powerful current of social and cultural change. We have been swimming with history, not against it.

And then along comes same-sex marriage. Or, rather, along come some yearning couples, plus a band of activists to support them, single-minded in their pursuit of marriage equality. They confuse ordinarily intelligent queers by purveying the line that full dignity, full respect, and full citizenship will come only when gays and lesbians have achieved unobstructed access to marriage.

It doesn't surprise me that, on balance, the results have been grim. Had we tried to devise a strategy that took advantage of the force of historical trends, we would, as a movement, have been pushing to further de-center and de-institutionalize marriage. Once upon a time, we did. In the 1980s and early 1990s, imaginative queer activists invented such things as "domestic partnership" and "second-parent adoption" as ways of recognizing the plethora of family arrangements that exist throughout the United States. AIDS activists pressed for such things as universal health insurance that would have decoupled perhaps the most significant benefit that marriage offers. (A great irony: universal health care, which has seemed so remote in the conservative era that Reagan ushered in, could more successfully have been fought for state-by-state than could same-sex marriage.)

I don't think it's too much to ask that our organizational leadership, especially at the national level, pursue intelligent strategies. Nor is it too much to ask that they have the courage to say "this isn't working" and make a major course correction. We're already going to have to live with the negative results of their misjudgments for a long time. Please stop throwing good money after bad. And, please, make history be something that works for us instead of racing into the wind against history.

Postscript: Since I drafted this essay, the Washington State Supreme Court has issued a ruling upholding the state's ban on same-sex marriage. Gay leaders have once again expressed shock and anger at the decision and have pledged to keep fighting for marriage equality. Fortunately, the same day as the Washington decision, a group of queer activists who are mostly outside the network of "mainstream" GLBT organizations have released a document, "Beyond Same-Sex Marriage: A New Strategic Vision for All Our Families and Relationships, " that calls for a shift in direction. Over 200 activists and intellectuals have signed it (full disclosure: I'm one of the signatories). Could this be a new beginning?

This piece originally appeared online at the Bilerico Project (bilerico.com) and in print with UltraViolet in late fall of 2009.

Against Equality, In Maine and Everywhere

Ryan Conrad

In the aftermath of the losing battle for gay marriage rights in Maine, many local queer and trans activists have been left wondering how we even got here in the first place. And the more troubling question is: who is going to clean up this mess? How did gay marriage become "the issue" in Maine and how did so many LGBTA folks get duped into making this campaign their top priority, emotionally, financially and otherwise, by the shallow rhetoric of equality? If we, as a radical queer community, are to prevent the de-prioritization and de-funding of critical queer and trans community issues/organizations/services, the campaign in Maine must be dissected and used as a case study to learn from. Our queerest futures depend on it!

Maine in Context:
Material Conditions/Political Positionings

Maine is one of the poorest states in the country with a majority of its manufacturing outsourced overseas and its agricultural industries struggling to keep up with the rising costs of doing business. The state ranks 43rd out of all states when measuring average annual income and has the 15th highest unemployment rate in the nation.[1] To say that the economy in Maine is struggling is an understatement, and employment/poverty is a major concern for working class queer and trans folks.

Maine is also the largest New England state covering an area greater than all the other New England states combined with a population about the same size as Rhode Island. Maine's overwhelmingly white population and most of its wealth is concentrated along the coast, particularly in the southern part of the state. As in many other states in the US, this creates a dichotomy of rural poor versus urban wealth that is often translated to conservative versus liberal. It's not that there aren't rich people from Boston buying second homes in the rural areas down east or abject poverty in small cities like Lewiston and Waterville, but the overwhelming trend points towards a paradigm of rural poverty in most of the state. Organizing a truly statewide campaign across such a large, rural, poor area is particularly challenging.

Under these material conditions queer and trans folks in Maine have been fighting for their lives. For over a decade the state struggled to pass and uphold an addendum to the state's human rights act that gave non-discrimination protections to LGBT folks in housing, employment and credit. The non-discrimination law, once vetoed by the governor after passing legislation in 1993 and overturned twice by referendum in 1998 and 2000, was finally upheld in referendum in 2005 by a narrow margin.[2] The stranglehold of the conservative Christian right appeared to be weakening over the last two decades, but the bitter taste of defeat at the polls in the past still hadn't left our mouths upon entering the gay marriage referendum.

Outside of the political arena, queer and trans folks in Maine have continued to face anti-queer violence in their communities, in their homes and on the streets of even the most gay friendly towns. The gruesome murder of Scott A. Libby in Raymond in 2009,[3] the gay bashing of a man in Portland to the point of unconsciousness in 2008,[4] and the complete destruction of two lesbians' home and car in Poland in 2006 serve as just a few examples.[5] They don't just want us to not get married, they want us dead!

This Wedding Cake is Rotten

Gays and lesbians of all ages are obsessing over gay marriage as if it's going to cure AIDS, stop anti-queer/anti-trans violence, provide all uninsured queers with health care, and reform racist immigration policies. Unfortunately, marriage does little more than consolidate even more power in the hands of already privileged gay couples engaged in middle class hetero-mimicry.

Let's be clear: the national gay marriage campaign is NOT a social justice movement. Gay marriage reinforces the for-profit medical industrial complex by tying access to health care to employment and relational status. Gay marriage does not challenge patent laws that keep poor/working class poz folks from accessing life-extending medications. Gay marriage reinforces the nuclear family as the primary support structure for youth even though nuclear families are largely responsible for queer teen homelessness, depression and suicide. Gay marriage does not challenge economic systems set up to champion people over property and profit. Gay marriage reinforces racist immigration laws by only allowing productive, "good", soon-to-be-wed, non-citizens in while ignoring the rights of migrant workers. Gay marriage simply has nothing to do with social justice.

An Opportunistic National Strategy

The national strategy for gay marriage is much larger and more insidious than most expect. Maine was used as a pawn in a much larger scheme to pressure the federal government to take up the issue. Even though LGBTQ-identified Mainers spoke loud and clear about their priorities at both the statewide symposium convened by the Maine Community Foundation's Equity Fund in 2007 and in a pre-election poll put out by the Family Affairs Newsletter in January 2009, somehow we still found ourselves in the midst of a $6 million dollar campaign for someone else's priority. The FAN found that nearly 70% of their readers did not identify marriage as their top priority issue[6] and the symposium's 4,000 word summary only mentions gay marriage in one sentence positively.[7] Gay marriage is mentioned twice in the document, but in the second instance it is referenced negatively by youth at the conference who saw the gay marriage issue as pressuring them to live up to unwanted heteronormative expectations.[8]

Most of the rights and privileges cited by the talking heads of the gay marriage movement are actually doled out by the Federal government and not individual states, thus the needed pressure from regional blocks on the federal government. These 1,138 rights are cited by the General Accounting Office of the United States Government and largely pertain to the transfer of property and money.[9] If Maine had won with the popular vote, there would have been a greater opportunity to push the federal government to move on the issue as an entire regional block would be able to apply more serious pressure than through the piecemeal process of states legislating in favor of gay marriage across the country here and there.

This national influence was seen in Portland on election night when both the executive director from the Human Rights Campaign (Joe Solmonese) and the National Gay and Lesbian Task Force (Rea Carey) showed up to give the crowd a pep talk. Even more telling was the $400,000 plus dollars contributed by the HRC and NGLTG combined, as well as in-kind staff time.[10] If the NGLTF or HRC were interested in improving the lives of queer and trans Mainers, they would have given this kind of funding to issues actually outlined as critical at the statewide symposium and not to a bunch of power-consolidating homo-politicos in Portland.

More money continued to roll in from other gay marriage groups in Massachusetts, Vermont, California, Colorado, Oregon and New Jersey;[11] all recent gay marriage winners or soon-to-be-pawns in the state-by-state game to pressure the feds, whether the issue is a local priority or not.

Following the Money

The gay-marriage campaign has been sucking up resources like a massive sponge, corralling everyone to give up their last dollar and free time, leaving little sustenance for other queer groups doing critical work in our communities. An Equality Maine campaign letter had the audacity to claim that gay marriage is "the fight for our lives." I wonder whose lives they are talking about, when AIDS service organizations and community health/reproductive clinics across the state have been tightening their belts and desperately trying to crunch numbers so that more queer folks don't end up unemployed, uninsured, or worse yet, dead. These organizations include clinics like Western Maine Community Action Health Services, AIDS service organizations like Down East AIDS Network, Eastern Maine AIDS Network, Maine AIDS Alliance, the Frannie Peabody Center, and queer/trans youth support groups like Out as I Want to Be, Outrageously Supportive, Outright L/A, and PRYSM.

In addition, over the last few years we have seen the Maine Speak Out Project and the Charlie Howard Memorial Library close their doors in Portland while the few remaining LGBT youth advocacy groups across the state scrounge just to keep their doors open after most of them folded in the late nineties. The Department of Education has also announced that it will no longer be funding HIV Prevention Outreach

Educators as of June 2010. A particularly horrifying scenario for the queer community here, as queer men account for 67% of people living with HIV in Maine.[12]

While essential services are disappearing, organizations are closing, and new gaps in services for aging LGBTQ folks are being identified, the marriage campaign in Maine is spending money with abandon. The No on 1 group spent close to $6 million dollars over the duration of the campaign,[13] taking in $1.4 million dollars in donations in the first three weeks of October alone.[14] In a state with a tanking economy, this kind of reckless spending on a single issue campaign that isn't even a top priority for most LGBT folks is blatant and unrestrained classism at its worst.

To put this budget in perspective, the largest funding source for LGBT organizations in the state is the Equity Fund, which only distributes $40,000 a year amongst the numerous LGBT applicant organizations.[15] At the current fiscal rate, it would take the Equity Fund about one hundred thirty five years to catch up with the spending accrued in one year by the Maine's gay marriage campaign. Imagine what kind of change could be made if that $6 million dollars was used to support organizational capacity building and programming of those organizations providing essential services and advocacy that the Equity Fund supports with their meager budget. This kind of long-term approach to advocating real change seems like an obvious preference to throwing money down the drain in single-issue legislative campaigns.

Cultural Change vs. Legislative Change

Changing a law in a book does much less to create an atmosphere of safety for queer and trans folks than long-term cultural change. In fact, in Maine the gay marriage law and referendum has conjured more reactionary anti-queer violence than before. This can be seen quite clearly in Maine where the platform for people to air their homophobic grievances became massively public. This overwhelming outpouring of homophobic vitriol via every kind of media outlet and public forum imaginable has had a terrible impact on LGBT youths' mental health in particular. One needs no further proof than volunteering at one of the few remaining queer and trans youth advocacy organizations in the poorer part of the state like I do in Androscoggin County. Here youth have been utterly demoralized, openly gay bashed in school and town newspapers, and some even banned from starting a Gay Straight

Alliance in their Somerset County High School because of homophobic school staff citing the gay marriage campaigns as too controversial.

The focus of this campaign was to win the referendum by getting out the vote in winnable parts of the state, ie. metro-Portland and the coast, leaving the already most vulnerable queers in the rural parts of the state to fend for themselves while the campaign drums up homophobic fervor across the inland counties. Those abandoned by the faux statewide campaign in the rural parts of the state have no support organizations to turn to once the campaign is over as they do not exist or barely do. Furthermore, even if gay marriage had passed, would it even be safe to get gay married in most of the state? Quite clearly, no. And again, power and privilege remain among those who already had them to begin with.

Some suggest that gay marriage is part of a progress narrative and that it is a step in the right direction towards more expansive social justice issues. This largely ignores a critique of power. Once privilege is doled out to middle class gay couples, are they going to continue on to fight against racist immigration policies, for universal health care, for comprehensive queer/trans inclusive sex education, or to free queers unjustly imprisoned during rabidly homophobic sex-abuse witch hunts?[16] Doubtful is an overstatement. It's more likely they will be enjoying summer vacations at an expensive bed and breakfast in Ogunquit while the rest of us are still trying to access basic rights like health care and freedom of movement. Let's be real: privilege breeds complacency.

Queer Futures Against Equality

The for/against dichotomy setup by the gay marriage movement and the homophobic legislative pandering of the Christian right is an absolute distraction.

If we are to imagine queer futures that don't replicate the same violence and oppression many of us experience on an everyday basis as queer and trans folks, we must challenge the middle class neo-liberal war machine known as the national gay marriage campaign. We must fight the rhetoric of equality and inclusion in systems of domination like marriage and the military, and stop believing that our participation in those institutions is more important than questioning those institutions legitimacy all together. We need to call out the national marriage campaign as opportunistic and parasitic. We must challenge their money mongering tactics to assure our local, truly community based

LGBT organizations aren't left financially high and dry while offering the few essential services to the most marginalized of our community. Let Maine be an early example of why we must continue to fight against equality.

1. U.S. Census Bureau, 2009 Statistical Abstract: State Rankings.
2. http://www.equalitymaine.org/the-issues/non-discrimination.
3. http://scottlibby.blogspot.com.
4. Suspect Sought in Alleged Hate Crime, *Portland Press Herald*, 10 September 2008, http://news.mainetoday.com/updates/032723.html.
5. Couple Calls Vandalism a Hate Crime, WGME 13, 19 July 2006, http://www.wmtw.com/news/9543231/detail.html?rss=port&psp=new.
6. Family Affairs Newsletter, Bangor, 15 January 2009.
7. LGBT Symposium 2007: Strengthening Communities, Building Alliances Summary Report, 2008.
8. Ibid.
9. General Accounting Office, Categories of Law Involving Marital Status, 1997, http://gao.gov/archive/1997/og97016.pdf.
10. Follow the Money, http://www.followthemoney.org/database/StateGlance/committee.phtml?c=3925.
11. Ibid.
12. Maine Comprehensive HIV/AIDS Prevention Plan 2004-2008, HIV Epidemiological Data Provided by Maine Bureau of Health, 2003.
13. Follow the Money, http://www.followthemoney.org/press/ReportView.phtml?r=404.
14. Miller, Kevin. Money fueling battle over gay marriage, *Bangor Daily News*, 24 October 2009.
15. Summary of Recent Grants from the Equity Fund 2008, http://www.mainecf.org/grants/recentgrants/equitygrants.aspx
16. Bernard Baran Justice Committee, http://www.freebaran.org.

Versions of this piece originally appeared on Queercents (queercents.com) and The Bilerico Project (bilerico.com) in May 2009.

Who's Illegal Now?: Immigration, Marriage, and the Violence of Inclusion

Yasmin Nair

If you spent any time at all this past summer walking down a busy street in a city like Chicago, you would have run into one of the countless young people representing the Human Rights Campaign (HRC). Without a doubt, he or she was wearing what seems to be the designated uniform of the legions of (paid) recruits for "marriage equality": an American Apparel t-shirt with the words "Legalize Gay" emblazoned across it.

If you were the sort of unthinking liberal/progressive towards whom this shirt was aimed, you would have nodded in assent and eagerly signed on to whatever petition/ membership drive was waved at you by the HRC representative. Yes, you would have thought, in your well-meaning if somewhat clueless and ahistorical way, we must "legalize gay." But anyone with a modicum of sense and, oh, a sense of history would have wondered, as I do: who, exactly, is illegal here? Does the admonition make either grammatical or political sense?

Are gays now illegal? Are the streets now filled with police roaming the streets in Humvees, guns drawn and mouths tightly clenched, looking for gays to throw into a giant gay gulag? Is it now forbidden to be a man who wears pink? Are men driven out of hairdressing salons and interior design firms? Are we now forbidden from watching *Glee*? I mean, no, really, who's illegal now?

As it turns out, the ubiquitous t-shirt (go to any gay event and the damn thing appears on at least a dozen torsos within spitting distance) has an interesting history, one that is implicated in the sordid machinations of the "marriage equality" movement and which shamelessly exploits the hard-won civil rights battles of this country.

The t-shirt first popped up into view immediately after the passage of Proposition 8 in California, and was featured on the AA website in a range of colors, including teal and pink (how gay!), with the words "Repeal Prop 8" directly below "Legalize Gay." The promotional material went on to say: "In the fall of 2008, Proposition 8 passed in California, striking down the legalization of same-sex marriage. Now the decision rests in the hands of California's Supreme Court, with state lawmakers declaring the vote unconstitutional. Equal rights for all— repeal Prop 8."

Now that prop 8 has been struck down, the slogan has become the unofficial motto of the HRC, which shamelessly pretends that it was originally crafted for it by AA when, in fact, what it means is that the current manifestation of the shirt as seen on its own website, with a tiny version of the HRC equals sign, was designed by AA. This is, of course, typical of the HRC which would, if it could, claim that it was there at the dawn of time when gays were created.

But the "Legalize Gay" t-shirt provides more than a catchy slogan for the "marriage equality" movement. The words serve to first perpetuate a fiction of illegality (we are to assume that "gay" is now "illegal") and then yoke marriage to both a domestic history of civil rights battles and the contentious issue of immigration. The specious connection to marriage is easy to locate, as we saw above, while the one to immigration is more complicated—but both are made in equally problematic ways.

The t-shirts are a variation on AA's "Legalize L.A" t-shirts, part of the company's attempt to market itself as an immigrant-rights-friendly entity. Founded in 1997 by Dov Charney, AA became famous for being the largest U.S. clothing manufacturer based entirely in this country. In other words, AA does not outsource its manufacturing, pays its workers between $11-$18 an hour, and claims to be sweatshop free. But the company is also anti-union—and management has reportedly gone about strenuously and aggressively busting any attempts to form one. Which begs the question: how can any corporation be worker-friendly and anti-union? In early 2010, AA was subjected to an Immigration and Customs Enforcement (ICE) raid on its workers, of whom 2,500 were found to be undocumented (ICE puts the number closer to 1,500). More recently, in the summer of 2010, AA has seen its profits drop steeply. Charney has blamed the company's financial woes on his loss of employees due to the ICE crackdowns. Predictions for AA's economic health are, at the time of this writing, dire.

Charney's woes hardly end at the business side of the corporation. He has, from the outset, been sharply criticized for what many consider sexist advertisements, featuring young and thin models in various enticing poses (how and why these are any different from what appears in the pages of *Vogue* magazine is a mystery that has never been addressed by his critics). More significantly, he has faced sexual harassment charges from former female employees. Through it all, Charney has managed to skate on his bad boy image but the allure of that reputation may be fading in light of his financial troubles. Sure, we like our bad boys—but we also want them to be *successful* bad boys.

AA was teetering towards a downslide around the time of Proposition 8, so it is not outlandish to assume that the "Legalize Gay" t-shirt was just one more way for it to curry favor with a population of consumers that most marketing experts define as upwardly mobile to well-off, buying into the stereotype that "gay" is a class identity unto itself.

The slogan "Legalize Gay" presents a visible and entirely fictitious suggestion that to be gay is illegal while simultaneously erasing the very troubling ways in which the undocumented labor that makes the t-shirts is literally rendered illegal. In fact: after Lawrence v. Texas, sodomy is no longer illegal. In 1991, U.S Attorney Janet Reno lifted the ban on gay and lesbian immigrants. While several states still lack explicit anti-discrimination laws against the LGBT population, to be gay is not illegal—you cannot be hauled away for being discovered as gay. Sure, gays and lesbians might not be allowed to marry in several states but this has not meant that those with otherwise unblemished records can no longer leave their houses, or buy cars, or keep their jobs.

Do people wearing this t-shirt have a clue what it really means to be illegal? To be, for instance, an "illegal alien" who gets swept up in an Immigration and Customs Enforcement raid and is deported soon thereafter? To be unable to travel freely because they lack the proper documentation? To pay for their school tuition and rent in cash because they lack social security numbers?

It is not just the undocumented whose lives are effectively erased by this t-shirt, but the millions who are being funneled into the prison industrial complex in order to increase its profits. According to Bob Libal, co-author of "Operation Streamline: Drowning Justice and Draining Dollars along the Rio Grande," Texas alone has diverted an estimated 1.2 billion federal dollars "into warehousing the undocumented in predominantly for-profit private jails and detention centers, while they await trial or serve sentences prior to deportation." Over the last decade or so, more of the undocumented are detained, often indefinitely, for non-violent and petty crimes, and the increased numbers inflate the perception that the undocumented are inherently criminal while expanding the prison industrial complex. The numbers have exploded because the PIC has been relentlessly creating new categories of "illegal aliens," and putting people in jail for longer periods of time.

The "Legalize Gay" t-shirt allows the wearer to smugly pose as "illegal" while cluelessly erasing the reality that millions are actually made illegal in the terms dictated by draconian laws around immigration and the prison industrial complex, which create new and ever-shifting categories of illegality for immigrants.

While the t-shirt erases the reality of immigration, "marriage equality" advocates are also attempting to appropriate the issue of immigration reform with a focus on the Uniting American Families Act (UAFA). Groups like Immigration Equality (IE) will pay scant atten   her matters which affect queer immigrants, like the now-lif   IIV-positive people or asylum on the basis of sexual orien   their slight attention to these serves as a smokescreen for their emphasis on the UAFA, a piece of legislation which essentially seeks to provide the benefits of marriage to gay and lesbian citizens and permanent residents and their non-citizen partners. Under U.S law, and under specific legal circumstances, a citizen or permanent resident is allowed to sponsor their spouse for immigration. Given that gay marriage is not federally recognized, gays and lesbians cannot do the same; the UAFA seeks to correct that by replicating the visa requirements for same-sex partners. It essentially substitutes the phrase "permanent partnership" for "spouse" wherever applicable in immigration law.

The UAFA was first introduced as the Permanent Partners Act of 2000 and eventually re-named, presumably to add more affect by evoking the specter of families torn apart. It has frequently died in committee but was recently galvanized by the situation of Shirley Tan and her family. Tan came here in 1986 as a tourist, and overstayed her visa in order to remain with her partner Jay Mercado who was, like her, originally from the Philippines. Mercado is currently a citizen, but Tan is still undocumented. They have been domestic partners for a while, according to a *People* article, and even wed in 2004. Tan gave birth to their twin sons who are both citizens. In 1995, Tan applied for asylum because, in 1979, according to her, a cousin shot her in the head and killed her mother and sister. In 2002, ICE (Immigration and Customs Enforcement) served Tan with an order of deportation, but the couple claim to never have received it. Finally, in 2009, ICE agents showed up at the couple's Pacifica California home and arrested her. At the time of this writing, Tan has been able to obtain stays on her deportation while she waits to hear about the fate of the UAFA.

Immigration Equality and other supporters of the UAFA have made Shirley Tan and her family members the poster children for a piece of legislation that, they claim, would guarantee that binational couples like the Tan-Mercados are able to stay together. In the process, they have continued to emphasize the sheer American-ness of Tan and her family (Her kids play soccer! She's a stay-at-home mom! She sings in the choir!) while, in not-so-subtle ways marking her as the preferable alternative to those *other* nasty "illegals." In the same *People* article, Rachel Tiven of IE was quoted as saying, "*They* are exactly the kinds of immigrants you want in this country." (emphasis mine) Right. The others can just rot in hell. You know the ones they mean—the day laborers who move from job to job, underpaid and overexploited; the low-paid workers who build suburban houses for us on the cheap as opposed to living in them; and so on.

As queer immigration rights activists or as people concerned with the same, our concerns should be with comprehensive immigration reform (CIR). The current immigration crisis has come about because the United States feeds on cheap labor and the exploitation of millions, the very people it chooses to dispose of quickly and crudely via the mechanisms of raids and deportations. It does this because it knows that there is more cheap labor to be had because of the conditions of "free trade" it has created, conditions that guarantee a breakdown in the economies of countries like Mexico. These conditions, in turn, guarantee the flow of people desperate to find a living here.

The UAFA does not change the paradigms of immigration and, in fact, completely ignores the issues of labor that have created the current crisis. It goes so far as to erase the domestic labor performed by women (or men) like Tan in favor of a fantasy narrative about the nuclear family with a single bread-winner. It fixates on an emotional and affective problem, posited as a problem of true love—what could be truer than decades of living together and children? It is a quick-fix solution for a privileged few and does nothing to address the larger economic crisis that is immigration in the United States.

The UAFA is now being presented as *the* immigration cause for LGBT people. But if queers are to speak about immigration in any form, we need to understand the larger context in which such bills operate. The UAFA will not benefit every gay and lesbian couple, and it will be a distraction from CIR. It makes a grand symbolic gesture, but it is also most likely an exercise in futility that will not, in fact, even benefit many binational couples. While it is not explicitly a marriage bill, it is in fact one that compels people to conjoin in the same way as married partners—but only if you have the economic resources.

For instance, if you or your partner entered the country illegally and without inspection, chances are that spousal sponsorship won't help anyway. But, and this is a huge complication that can enter even for straight couples: under certain circumstances, even a spouse can be subject to a 10-year ban, which means that she/he will have to return to the country of origin and not return for a decade.

Is your head spinning yet?

What it comes down to is this: under very narrow circumstances, Shirley Tan's case could be replicated in a straight binational marriage, but each case is unique and not all straight marriages are automatic routes to citizenship. Tan's case is somewhat complicated because she also sought to gain asylum, a petition that was denied. But even if all things were equal, there is the issue of economics. The UAFA deems it necessary that the sponsoring partner show proof of ample resources, which leaves poorer people out of the picture. In fact, IE and HRC representatives at an immigration conference I attended spoke about the need to show the economic costs if binational couples decided to leave the United States for a country like Canada that recognizes their relationships—they might just up and leave! This is the supposed trump card—if gay and lesbian couples are not allowed to be together, several of them with lucrative businesses will just take them to countries like Canada. So there.

Of course, if you don't have the resources, tough luck. And good lawyers who won't just take your money and run can be hard to find. In addition, the speed with which your immigration application goes through the system depends a lot on your country of origin. What most people do not know is that immigration law is incredibly arcane and subject to the whims of issues as fickle as shifting relations between the United States and other countries. So, if your partner is from a country like, say the Netherlands or France, the chances are that your passage will be easier. If you are from Iran or Pakistan –well, how easy do think your application will be?

What is also left out of the whole spouse/permanent partnership issue is the fact that such relationships are also likely to be rife with abuse. The UAFA specifically requires that partners demonstrate financial interdependency. Partnerships, like straight marriages, will be subject to a two-year period during which much of the power rests with the sponsoring partner. If you are on your spouse's H1-B (on an H-4, the visa which allows you to enter the country as a "spousal dependent"), you cannot get a social security number and you cannot apply for jobs; in many states you will not even be permitted a valid driver's license. *The Hindu*, an Indian newspaper, has written about the abuse of women on their husbands' H-4 visas. The abuse is so widespread that immigration rights activists are currently trying to reform the process so that the dependent spouse might gain some measure of dignity and

independence. Is this the kind of   ve feminist queers fought
for? Do we seriously believe th   e love between gays and
lesbian couples makes it impossible for such abuse to occur?

Do we really think love will be enough?

So where does this leave Shirley Tan and others like her? It absolutely
makes sense that we agitate on their behalf. If there is a petition to sign,
sign it. If there is a march in your town, go ahead and march. At the
very least, the law needs to change so that it is more flexible and grants
people like Tan the leeway to be in the country they now call home.
But, at the same time, ask yourself, as either a queer or a straight
citizen, about those millions of undocumented who don't have the
resources to leave. Consider those millions of undocumented
immigrants who might be in binational relationships but whose families
are not considered ideal because they lack the money and respectability
that the law demands.

The fact is that the UAFA doesn't really stand much of a chance
because Republicans and Democrats alike worry that it's a way of
writing gay marriage into federal law. And, let us be blunt about it: it is,
even if its supporters insist otherwise. This is marriage by another
name, and it demands that couples tie themselves to a shockingly
retrograde form of economic dependency which feminists have long
been fighting against. I happen to be against gay marriage for reasons
that have to do with my position on the left, but there are plenty of
people on the right who do not want it for different reasons. If the
UAFA is forced into CIR, there's a chance that CIR itself will suffer
because this legislation might well become the proverbial straw that
breaks the camel's back as far as these conservatives are concerned.
Gays and lesbians in binational couples and their supporters will be
able to make an emotional and symbolic point about the discrimination
they suffer, but the costs to CIR may be irreparable. So, go ahead and
protest for Shirley Tan and others like her. But if you cannot or will not
protest on behalf of the millions of others who don't fit the cozy and
unrealistic idea of "family" as well, don't protest at all.

This piece originally appeared online as a blog at queerkidssaynomarriage.wordpress.com in October 2009. This version includes a note from both the authors after the original piece.

Queer Kids of Queer Parents Against Gay Marriage!

Martha Jane Kaufman and Katie Miles

It's hard for us to believe what we're hearing these days. Thousands are losing their homes, and gays want a day named after Harvey Milk. The U.S. military is continuing its path of destruction, and gays want to be allowed to fight. Cops are still killing unarmed black men and bashing queers, and gays want more policing. More and more Americans are suffering and dying because they can't get decent health care, and gays want weddings. What happened to us? Where have our communities gone? Did gays really sell out that easily?

As young queer people raised in queer families and communities, we reject the liberal gay agenda that gives top priority to the fight for marriage equality. The queer families and communities we are proud to have been raised in are nothing like the ones transformed by marriage equality. This agenda fractures our communities, pits us against natural allies, supports unequal power structures, obscures urgent queer concerns, abandons struggle for mutual sustainability inside queer communities and disregards our awesomely fabulous queer history.

Children of queers have a serious stake in this. The media sure thinks so, anyway. The photographs circulated after San Francisco mayor Gavin Newsom's 2004 decision to marry gay couples at City Hall show men exchanging rings with young children strapped to their chests and toddlers holding their moms' hands as city officials lead them through vows. As Newsom runs for governor these images of children and their newly married gay parents travel with him, supposedly expressing how deeply Newsom cares about families: keeping them together, ensuring their safety, meeting their needs. These photos, however, obscure very real aspects of his political record that have torn families apart: his disregard for affordable housing, his attacks on welfare, his support for increased policing and incarceration that separate parents from children and his new practice of deporting minors accused—not convicted—of crimes. As young people with queer parents we are not proud of the "family values" politic put forth by these images and the marriage equality campaign. We don't want gay marriage activism conducted in our name—we realize that it's hurting us, not helping us.

We think long-term monogamous partnerships are valid and beautiful ways of structuring and experiencing family, but we don't see them as any more inherently valuable or legitimate than the many other family structures. We believe in each individual and family's right to live their queer identity however they find meaningful or necessary, including when that means getting married. However, the consequences of the fight for legal inclusion in the marriage structure are terrifying. We're seeing queer communities fractured as one model of family is being hailed and accepted as the norm, and we are seeing queer families and communities ignore and effectively work against groups who we see as natural allies, such as immigrant families, poor families, and families suffering from booming incarceration rates. We reject the idea that any relationship based on love should have to register with the state. Marriage is an institution used primarily to consolidate privilege, and we think real change will only come from getting rid of a system that continually doles out privilege to a few more, rather than trying to reform it. We know that most families, straight or gay, don't fit in with the standards for marriage, and see many straight families being penalized for not conforming to the standard the government has set: single moms trying to get on welfare, extended family members trying to gain custody, friends kept from being each other's legal representatives. We have far more in common with those straight families than we do with the kinds of gay families that would benefit from marriage. We are seeing a gay political agenda become single-issue to focus on marriage and leave behind many very serious issues such as social, economic, and racial justice.

How the marriage agenda is leaving behind awesome queer history.

We're seeing the marriage equality agenda turn its back on a tradition of queer activism that began with Stonewall and other fierce queer revolts and that continued through the AIDS crisis. Equality California keeps on sending us videos of big, happy, gay families, and they're making us sick: gay parents pushing kids on swings, gay parents making their kids' lunches, the whole gay family safe inside the walls of their own homes. Wait a second, is it true? It's as if they've found some sort of magical formula: once you have children, your life instantly transforms into a scene of domestic bliss, straight out of a 1950s movie. The message is clear. Instead of dancing, instead of having casual sex, instead of rioting, all of the "responsible" gays have gone and had children. And now that they've had children, they won't be bothering you at all anymore. There's an implicit promise that once gays get their rights, they'll disappear again. Once they can be at home with the kids, there's no reason for them to be political, after all!

Listening to this promise, we're a bit stunned. Whoever said domesticity wasn't political? Wasn't it just a few years ago that the feminists taught us that the personal is political? That cooking, cleaning, raising children and putting in countless hours of physical, emotional, and intellectual labor should not mean withdrawing from the public sphere or surrendering your political voice? After all, we were raised by queers who created domestic lives that were always politically engaged, who raised kids and raised hell at the same time. What makes Equality California think that an official marriage certificate is going to make us any less loud and queer? Oh wait. We remember. It's that sneaky thing about late liberal capitalism: its promise of formal rights over real restructuring, of citizenship for those who can participate in the state's economic plan over economic justice for all. Once you have your formal rights (like a marriage license), you can participate in the market economy and no longer need a political voice. Looking around at the world we live in, we're unconvinced.

We're also seeing another alarming story surface: If gays are ready to get married and have children, the AIDS crisis must be over! Gay men shaped up after AIDS hit, or at least the smart ones did. Those responsible enough to survive realized that they wanted children, and promptly settled down into relationships that were monogamous and that, presumably, carried no risk of HIV contraction. Come on. We reject all the moralizing about parenthood, responsibility, and sexual practice that goes on in this story. Besides the obvious fact that the AIDS crisis is not over, in the US or abroad, we realize that parenthood and non-monogamy aren't mutually exclusive. The gay marriage movement wants us to believe that you need a sperm donor or an adoption agency to have children, but we know that there are more ways to make queer families than any of us can imagine. We refuse the packaged and groomed history that writes out the many HIV+ individuals in our lives and communities who are living healthily, loving in monogamous and non-monogamous relationships and raising children. We challenge our queer communities to remember our awesomely radical history of building families and raising children in highly political, inventive, and non-traditional ways.

How marriage equality fractures our community and pits us against our strongest allies.

We believe that the argument for gay marriage obscures the many structural, social, and economic forces that break families apart and take people away from their loved ones. Just for starters, there's the explosion in incarceration levels, national and international migration for economic survival, deportation, unaffordable housing, and lack of access to drug rehabilitation services. The argument for gay marriage also ignores the economic changes and cuts to social services that make it nearly impossible for families to stay together and survive: welfare cuts, fewer after school programs, less public housing, worse medical care, not enough social workers, failing schools, the economic crisis in general.

We choose solidarity with immigrant families whom the state denies legal recognition and families targeted by prisons, wars, and horrible jobs. We reject the state violence that separates children from parents and decides where families begin and end, drawing lines of illegality through relationships. We see this as part of a larger effort on the part of the state to control our families and relationships in order to preserve a system that relies on creating an underclass deprived of security in order to ensure power for a few. We know that everyone has a complex identity, and that many queer families face separation due to one or more of the causes mentioned here, now or in the future. We would like to see our queer community recognize marriage rights as a short-term solution to the larger problem of the government's disregard for the many family structures that exist. As queers, we need to take an active role in exposing and fighting the deeper sources of this problem. We won't let the government decide what does and does not constitute a family.

The way that the marriage agenda phrases its argument about healthcare shows just how blind it is to the needs of the queer community. It has adopted marriage as a single-issue agenda, making it seem like the queer community's only interest in healthcare is in the inclusion of some members of two person partnerships in the already exclusive healthcare system. Health care is a basic human right to which everyone is entitled, not one that should be extended through certain kinds of individual partnerships. We know this from queer history, and if we forget it, we will continue to let our community live in danger. The question of universal healthcare is urgent to queers because large groups of people inside our communities face incredible difficulty and violence receiving medical care, such as trans people who seek hormone treatment or surgery, people who are HIV positive, and queer and trans youth who are forced to live on the street. Instead of equalizing access to health care, marriage rights would allow a small group of people who have partnered themselves in monogamous configurations to receive care. If we accept the marriage agenda's so-called solution, we'll leave out most of our community.

Perhaps because the gay marriage movement has forgotten about the plurality and diversity of queer communities and queer activism, it has tried to gloss over its shortcomings by appropriating the struggles of other communities. We reject the notion that "gay is the new black," that the fight for marriage equality is parallel to the fight for civil rights, that queer rights and rights for people of color are mutually exclusive. We don't believe that fighting for inclusion in marriage is the same as fighting to end segregation. Drawing that parallel erases queer people of color and makes light of the structural racism that the civil rights movement fought against. The comparison is made as if communities of color, and black communities in particular, now enjoy structural equality. We know that's not true. We would like to see a queer community that, rather than appropriating the narrative of the civil rights movement for its marriage equality campaign, takes an active role in exposing and protesting structural inequality and structural racism.

Rather than choosing to fight the things that keep structural racism intact, the liberal gay agenda has chosen to promote them. The gay agenda continually fights for increased hate crimes legislation that would incarcerate and execute perpetrators of hate crimes. We believe that incarceration destroys communities and families, and does not address why queer bashings happen. Increased hate crimes legislation would only lock more people up. In a country where entire communities are ravaged by how many of their members get sent to jail, where prisons are profit-driven institutions, where incarceration only creates more violence, we won't accept anything that promotes prison as a solution. Our communities are already preyed upon by prisons—trans people, sex workers, and street kids live with the constant threat of incarceration. We believe that real, long-term solutions are found in models of restorative and transformative justice, and in building communities that can positively and profoundly deal with violence. We challenge our queer communities to confront what we are afraid of rather than locking it up, and to join members of our community and natural allies in opposing anything that would expand prisons.

The gay marriage agenda also supports the expansion of the army, seemingly forgetting about all of the ways that the army creates and maintains violence and power. The gay marriage agenda fights to abolish the "don't ask don't tell" policy, promoting the military's policy and seeking inclusion. We've thought long and hard about this, and we can't remember liking anything that the US military has done in a really long time. What we do remember is how the military mines places where poor people and people of color live, taking advantage of the lack of opportunities that exist for kids in those communities and convincing them to join the army. We think it's time that queers fight the army and the wars it is engaged in instead of asking for permission to enter.

Marriage doesn't promise real security.

As the economy collapses, as the number of Americans without a job, without healthcare, without savings, without any kind of social security net increases, it's easy to understand how marriage has become an instant cure-all for some. Recognizing that many in our community have lived through strained or broken relationships with their biological families, through the darkest days of the AIDS epidemic in the United States, through self-doubt about and stigmatization of their relationships, we understand where the desire for the security promised by marriage comes from. However, we see the promotion of gay marriage as something that tries to put a band-aid over deeper sources of insecurity, both social and economic. With marriage, the state is able to absolve itself of responsibility for the well-being of its citizens, as evidenced by the HRC's argument that with gay marriage, the state could kick more people off of welfare. If the HRC got its way, the queers who do not want, or are not eligible for, marriage would be even less secure than before. We're frightened by the way the marriage agenda wants to break up our community in this way, and we're committed to fighting any kind of politics that demonizes poor people and welfare recipients. We challenge our queer communities to build a politics that promotes wealth redistribution. What if, rather than donating to the HRC campaign, we pooled our wealth to create a community emergency fund for members of our community who face foreclosure, need expensive medical care or find themselves in any other economic emergency? As queers, we need to take our anger, our fear, and our hope and recognize the wealth of resources that we already have, in order to build alternative structures. We don't need to assimilate when we have each other.

We're not like everyone else.

Everywhere we turn, it seems like someone wants us to support gay marriage. From enthusiastic canvassers on the street to liberal professors in the academy, from gay lawyers to straight soccer moms, there's someone smiling at us, eager to let us know how strongly they support our "right to marry," waiting for what should be our easy affirmation. And there seems to be no space for us to resist the agenda that has been imposed upon us. We're fed up with the way that the gay marriage movement has tried to assimilate us, to swallow up our families, our lives, and our lovers into its clean-cut standards for what queer love, responsibility, and commitment should look like. We reject the idea that we should strive to see straight family configurations reflected in our families. We're offended by the idea that white, middle-class gays—rather than genderqueers, poor people, single moms, prisoners, people of color, immigrants without papers, or anyone whose life falls outside of the norm that the state has set—should be our "natural" allies. We refuse to feel indebted or grateful to those who have decided it's time for us to be pulled out from the fringe and into the status quo. We know that there are more of us on the outside than on the inside, and we realize our power.

We write this feeling as if we have to grab our community back from the clutches of the gay marriage movement. We're frightened by its path and its incessant desire to assimilate. Believe it or not, we felt incredibly safe, happy, taken care of, and fulfilled with the many queer biological and chosen parents who raised us without the right to marry. Having grown up in queer families and communities we strongly believe that queers are not like everyone else. Queers are sexy, resourceful, creative, and brave enough to challenge an oppressive system with their lifestyle. In the ways that our families might resemble nuclear, straight families, it is accidental and coincidental, something that lies at the surface. We do not believe that queer relationships are the mere derivatives of straight relationships. We can play house without wanting to be straight. Our families are tangled, messy and beautiful—just like so many straight families who don't fit into the official version of family. We want to build communities of all kinds of families, families that can exist—that do exist—without the recognition of the state. We don't believe that parenting is cause for an end to political participation. We believe that nurturing the growth, voice and imagination of children as a parent, a family and a community is a profoundly radical act. We want to build networks of accountability and dependence that lie outside the bounds of the government, the kinds of networks that we grew up in, the kinds of networks that we know support single-parent families, immigrant families, families who have members in the military or in prison, and all kinds of chosen families. These families, our families, work through our collective resources, strengths, commitments, and desires, and we wouldn't change them for anything.

*   *   *

The above essay was written in October 2009. The marriage equality movement was gaining steam in advance of the National Equality March and we were frustrated by the way images of children with gay parents were being used in the media. When we first shared our essay, we never expected our words to spread so quickly or so far. It was written for our friends and fellow activists, and we had no idea what a large audience would read it. Since sharing this essay, our relationship to it has changed, in different ways for both of us. Below are first Katie's and then Martha's words about our relationship to the essay.

Since we shared the essay, we've heard a lot of generous and smart feedback from people who see gay marriage as very important for their families, emotionally and otherwise. We know that for many people, marriage, and the benefits it can give, can be a form of survival. We believe that people can experience an immediate need for the benefits marriage would provide and a simultaneous hope for more expansive solutions.

When we wrote about solidarity with other communities, we did so knowing that no lines exist between all of these communities, that all of us are members of more than one community, that our communities bleed into others, that they are all inextricably connected. Since writing the essay, though, both of us have become uncomfortable with using the term "solidarity." We don't want to mark out the groups with whom we should be strategically sharing power as separate from us, because we know that groups tend to overlap in identity. We often find that when we claim "solidarity" with one group or another, the use of that word obscures a more personal connection we have to the struggle in which we're engaged.

We see queerness as fundamentally about honoring and validating relationships built on love and an individuals' right to build the lives they want for their bodies, desires and needs. Because of this, we see many social justice struggles as intrinsically queer, and as crucial for queer individuals and communities. Queer struggles throughout history have shown us how imaginative and creative good, effective organizing is—and that is why we are excited, not resigned, about all of the possibilities we have as queers. It isn't that we think there's not enough energy for anything more than one fight—it's that we think that queers, as people who occupy all sorts of places that aren't even supposed to exist, have the power to build activism that can truly challenge the structures of power, and that is a part of a larger activism fought by all who exist outside of formal recognition.

-Katie Miles

The idea of struggling to fit my extensive, complex and tangled family into a model focusing exclusively on two primary parents has always been absurd to me. My brother and I have always been confused by school assignments that required us to draw our family tree. How were we supposed to fit two moms and dad into the space for two parents? How was I supposed to organize the branches generationally when my moms were 17 years apart and my aunt only 11 years older than me? Katie and I have both had more than two parental figures in our lives and know that many others around us have as well. Our families blur into communities, and we have benefited from many meaningful and supportive bonds that are not represented by either the conventional or the Marriage Equality movement's idea of marriage. In our first publication of this statement, we rejected the idea that any relationship based on love should have to register with the state to gain legitimacy.

Since our essay went out, however, I've heard a lot of smart and honest criticism from people who find it emotionally meaningful to be able to get state validation for their queer family structure. I had never considered the validation offered by the state meaningful, perhaps because I grew up in a queer family and community and have found support for my queer desires and identity from a young age regardless of state recognition. I now recognize the extent to which, for many queers (regardless of the environment in which they grew up and how queer friendly it was), the self-definition and emotional security offered by state recognition of a relationship can be important.

Many people responded to our essay defensively about their choice to get married. This confused me. Was our piece provocative? Offensive? How had we put people who should be our natural partners on the defense? I realized then, the extent to which our language could alienate people we wanted to convince. I realized that a great deal of what I wrote came from a place of anger: anger at the government for not recognizing my family, anger at my communities for fighting for gay marriage as though my family was invisible, and anger at the gay marriage movement for relentlessly inviting me to join without realizing they were leaving out my family structure. I know that writing from a place of anger stirs up anger and defensiveness in other people. I hope to move beyond the angry language in this statement towards open words that will encourage readers to identify rather than turn defensive. I choose the word "identify" with care. I actually think that everyone has a personal connection to the argument in our essay. Everyone has a messy family that extends beyond what the state can validate. Let's make space for all of our relationships to count.

In addition to realizing that a lot of our essay came from a place of anger, I've also realized that there is also some binary language in the essay that I am no longer comfortable with. Statements about what will "help" or "hurt" us, and who is on the "outside" or the "inside" fail to reflect the complex ways gay marriage both helps and hurts my family, how it simultaneously includes and excludes us.

Several months after we first wrote our essay, we were quoted in a *New York Times* article. The author quoted a number of younger queer-spawns who spoke out in favor of gay marriage. Reading the article, I was reminded suddenly of a press statement I gave at age 14, very much along the same lines as these younger queer spawns. The more I consider this personal shift, the less I see my fourteen-year-old self or any of the younger queer-spawns in the article as standing in opposition to me. I see the impulse to ask the state to validate your family and the impulse to ask for a more expansive solution as two sides of the same coin: a challenge to the government for not understanding how families actually form.

While filling in family trees was difficult for my brother and me, I know it will only be more complicated for my baby sister who has 2 moms, 2 dads and a sister 20 years older than she is. After too many years of being asked to do this assignment, a few summers ago I finally revolted. Instead of a family tree, I created a family vine. I drew myself surrounded by all of the most important people in my life. Everyone was connected, but by winding branches instead of top-to-bottom limbs. It reflected a reality about every family I've ever encountered: we are messy and complicated. I'm writing this now with the hope that we can move beyond a vision of marriage toward a world that recognizes that complexity and sustains and honors those of us who grow and thrive within it.

-Martha Jane Kaufman

This piece was published in the October 2009 issue of Maximum RocknRoll and online at the Bilerico Proejct (bilerico.com).

Why gay marriage IS the End of the World (or the queer world, at least)

Mattilda Bernstein Sycamore

These days, lesbian soccer moms and gay military intelligence experts are all over the media, whether sermonizing in op-eds, befriending the liberal intelligentsia, or speaking softly to closeted cable news anchors: We. Are. Just. Like. You.

Supposedly gay people have made lots of progress, and that's why the only issues we hear about involve marriage, gays in the military, gay cops, adoption, ordination into the priesthood, hate crimes legislation, and unquestioning gentrification and consumerism—please, stop me before I choke on my own vomit! In honor of the Maximum Rocknroll queer issue, it's time to pull together a gang of queer troublemakers to tear this assimilationist agenda to shreds, okay?

Here's the cast of characters:

Hilary Goldberg is a San Francisco-based filmmaker currently in the finishing stages of recLAmation, the definitive movie about reclaiming Los Angeles from Los Angeles, and oh are we waiting! **Yasmin Nair** is a Chicago activist who delivers delicious rants about the war against single people, the tyranny of religion, fake immigration reform, and bachelorette parties with equal fervor and finesse. **Gina Carducci** throws Switch, New York City's only monthly "genderqueer / women / trans BDSM party"—she also fetishizes film, and is currently working on All That Sheltering Emptiness, a devastating short experimental film created in collaboration with your host for this splashy article.

*   *   *

MBS: I don't know about you, but have you noticed that freshly mined, blood-drenched South African diamonds are the new accessory for the gay elite, or they might as well be with how much the gaysbian "LGBT" agenda has become nothing but marriage marriage marriage— oh, and maybe a little bit of marriage with that marriage, thank you! Many of us grew up experiencing the lovely embrace of marriage or its aftermath, so we, and most queers, certainly know a lot about how marriage is, and has always been a central place for beating up, raping and abusing women, children, queers, and transpeople. And, even better—getting away with it! What are the other problems with marriage, and the gay marriage agenda in particular?

HG: I was at a protest against HIV budget cuts in California, but only four other people were there. because the rest of the gaysbians had done their recommended yearly protest allowance for gay marriage a few months prior. And what is the point of marriage if everyone is sick or dead, how do you register for that—at cemeteries and Pottery Barn? Wow, that makes me think of health care—remember health care? Something universal-based, not privilege-shaped?

YN: Yeah, I don't get why a community of people who have historically been fucked over by their families and the state now consists of people who want those exact same institutions to validate their existence. I think marriage is the gay Prozac, the drug of choice for gaysbians today: It makes them forget that marriage isn't going to give everyone health care, it won't give us a subsistence wage, it won't end all these fucked up wars that are killing people everywhere else. I wish I could say that gay marriage is like Viagra, but alas it's actually making us forget about sex so that metaphor won't work.

MBS: Speaking of sex and metaphors, let's move on to gays in the military. It's time to forget about opposing all these bloody US colonial wars, we just want to throw on those humpy battle fatigues so we can go abroad to kill people and get away with it, right? U-S-A! Can we say that again? U-S-A! Okay, so obviously the real answer is the end of the US military, not rainbow Humvees. Anything to add?

HG: Let us not forget the Gay Bomb — much like the acid tests the CIA performed in the '50s and '60s, if that technology fell into savvy hands we could open some serious doors of perception to end the military industrial complex with some good old fashioned loving.

GC: Oh, but military service is the best way to break down gay stereotypes and homophobia! The more we kill kill kill, the more respect we get from our country— we serve our country too! We are a valuable contribution! Show them you know how to be a man!

YN: It's time for us to call out the "gay patriots" as the enablers of U.S imperialism. Has anyone else noticed that the public faces of Don't Ask Don't Tell tend to be relatively privileged and from the officer class? And that the stories go like this: "Oh, no, he was an educated Harvard graduate who spoke four languages in which to colonize other countries, and we let him go!" One of the funniest photographs I ever saw was of a rally in downtown Chicago. A gay Army vet stood pontificating about needing to be recognized by the US military. Right behind him, his friends held up an anti-war slogan banner with the words, "US Out of Iraq." I wondered: Now, does that mean just the non-gay soldiers? Do the gay soldiers get to stay behind and kick the ass and blow the limbs off darkies?

MBS: Speaking of darkies, let's move on to adoption—if Madonna, Brad Pitt and Angelina, and any other jetsetter can run around the world in search of the cutest kids in the countries most devastated by transnational corporate violence, and then snatch those kids up and hold them in their arms, how will gay people compete? We all need kids, right? Kids are the next big thing! How do you feel about the issue of gay adoption, and child-rearing in general, as a central preoccupation of the so-called "movement?"

HG: Why don't Madonna and Angelina, in their gay wisdom, adopt some adult queer artists and activists instead? For a fraction of what they spend on a handful of appropriated transnational youths, they could adopt queer artists en masse, and foster a global queer trust fund for the movement. No need for nannies and we'd love them even more than their children, and could be just as dependent, if not more so. Average gay couples could do the same thing, direct their money towards something more expansive and useful than a handbag—I mean a gaybie. I'm thinking of a website that pairs queer artists with gay couples who have big hearts to share their love and help.

GC: Yeah, no need for pacifiers, no need to push us around in strollers, and you don't have to wait nine months for us. We're right here! Mommy!!!!

YN: If you're white, beautiful little blonde children are the best, because then you'll look like a normal and natural family. But adopting one can be next to impossible! Little brown babies make the best gay accessories. Although, like every gay fashion accessory, babies have shifted in trends. I think Mongolian babies are now much more hip. Central and South American countries were once popular, maybe NAFTA opened up free trade in cute Latin babies! Until they discovered that some of those babies were most likely kidnapped. Awkward. They may not have those pesky rules in Mongolia. Of course, if you can adopt an HIV+ African baby whose mother is still around to waste away in the last throes of the disease, so that you can show the world what you rescued the baby from, all the better. Why is it that lesbians generally give birth but gay men usually adopt?

MBS: It's because gay men are busy studying for the priesthood. I know you've been studying hard too! Of course, one of the central demands of early gay liberation was the end to organized religion and all of its layers of violence, but that's old news. What do you all think about the issue of "LGBT" people becoming powerbrokers within organized religion?

HG: It makes me cry blood. The only atonement gays should be thinking about is a nice bondage scene. And the last time I interacted with organized religion, a drag queen nun, in full make-up, yelled at me to get into a degrading gender-enforced line at a corporatized "pride" event colonized by so called do-gooders. Fuck her and the rest of organized religion.

MBS: Oh—and let's not forget the holy grail of the gay movement, hate crimes legislation! Because if you shoot those goddamn homophobes twice, that'll really teach them a lesson—the electric chair will end homophobia! Seriously, hate crimes legislation does nothing but put more money, energy, and resources into the hands of the notoriously racist, classist, misogynist, homophobic and transphobic criminal so-called "justice" system. But then they trick us into thinking that hate crimes legislation will keep us safe. What is hate crimes legislation keeping us safe from?

HG: It keeps us safe from long-term solution-based healing. It's a real time saver, so we can focus on earning money instead of focusing on root causes of hatred. We can continue to own property and assimilate into larger society by avoiding any real discourse around the source of the hate, and perpetuate it instead, while upholding that pillar of community, the greatest benefactor of the hates crimes bills—oh-so-thriving, even in economic turmoil...Private Prison Business.

YN: Hate crimes legislation keeps us safe from the silly delusion that the justice system should actually work fairly for everybody, not just gays and defined "minorities." After all, a justice system that actually provides justice seems, well, just ever so 1970s and sweetly retrograde, darling. All bell bottoms and compassion. Hate crimes legislation keeps us from a world where people might actually have a chance to show that they have moved on from their mistakes, by locking them up for perpetuity. And it keeps us believing that letting people spend their lives in violent prisons where they're likely to be raped and beaten every day is somehow a way to... end anti-gay violence. Huh?

MBS: Speaking of anti-gay violence, let's move on to talking about the national institutions that drive this wonderful inclusive agenda. We'll start with everyone's favorite diamond merchant: HRC, the Human Rights Campaign. Also known as Helping Right-Wingers Cope, or Homogenous Ruling Class—what else are they good for?

GC: Harvesting Righteous Caucasians. Hiring Riot Cops.

YN: Press Releases. HRC can turn out a press release on a dime. Oh, and they're great at taking credit for every "gay agenda" item, through said press releases, whether or not they had anything to do with the action. So, yeah, cocktail parties and lobby days. HRC is really good at going to cocktail parties and hobnobbing with the rich and important.

MBS: Of course, HRC also likes to keep trans people out of so-called employment nondiscrimination legislation, and to make any hideous corporation look good, as long as they like HRC's press releases. Then there's NGLTF, the National Gay Lesbian Task Force. They're especially talented at recruiting well-meaning college students, and turning them into nonprofit office drones—Creating Change, their annual conference, is a great launching pad into the nonprofit industry, and a job at NGLTF is sure to get you more lucrative foundation work in the future—what else is NGLTF good for?

YN: For creating the illusion that the battle royale between Democrats and Republicans actually means anything. And for perpetuating the idea that there are no alternatives to either. For pretending that a few days of a conference filled with words like "organizing" and "social" and "progressive" actually changes much. For pretending that using the word "progressive" over and over again will a) actually make that stupid word mean anything b) make us believe that their support of marriage, hate crimes legislation, and repealing Don't Ask Don't Tell does not make them conservative.

GC: NGLTF is good for creating robots who are stuck repeating, "Do you have a moment for trans rights? Do you have a moment for trans rights?" And asking why why why why can you not come to our office for hours of volunteer calling calling calling and repeating what we tell you to think and say, "Why can't you make the time for trans rights? Why?" Two of these robots were harassing myself and a group of friends once and I was just waiting for my trans friend to say, "If you really want to know, I need a little time to recover from trying to overdose and kill myself last week." And for the robots to ask, "Why? It's trans rights."

MBS: Oh, and I love the Gay Lesbian Alliance Against Defamation, or GLAAD—I think they should be called SAAD, the Straight Alliance Against Defamation, since most of what they do involves giving awards to straight people for not saying "faggot" too much. What else are they good for?

YN: Being very confused, mostly. And whining. A lot. I think Bruno confused the hell out of them: "We object to this movie. We think. It's a set of offensive stereotypes. Although the lead character is so over the top, he couldn't even possibly be a stereotype. But wait, we live to be offended. Cohen's not gay. And he makes fun of gays. Even though he also makes fun of homophobes. Wait, are we offended? Or not? It's so hard to tell, because we have no sense of humor or logic. Even the gays are sick of us. Can we call that homophobia?"

MBS: Then there's the juicy Lambda Legal Defense Fund—fighting for our rights, one marriage at a time...

YN: Lambda might be scariest of the lot, because they're mostly lawyers who know how to twist any inane, conservative, retrograde idea like gay marriage into some kind of sterling social justice cause—and they do that by drowning us in legalese. I once watched Camilla Taylor, a Lambda power attorney in Chicago, spend an hour talking about the legal ins and outs of Prop 8. By the end of the hour, I was so stupefied by boredom that I was almost ready to sign on to gay marriage—just to get out of the room. There was, of course, not one word about whether marriage ought to be the way to gain any rights in the first place.

MBS: That's right—remember that the fight against anti-gay Proposition 8 in California that those marriage morons lost actually cost more than any other ballot measure in California history! Those maniacal marriage organizations spent $40 million on that shit—can you imagine what we would have if they took that $40 million and fought for single payer universal health care, or built an enormous queer youth shelter in San Francisco or Sacramento, Fresno or San Diego? With the leftovers, we could create a collectively run, all-ages, 24-hour sex club with free vegan food, knock-you-down music of all types, free massage, acupuncture, and healthcare for all needs, as well as a special area for training people in squatting and neighborhood redecoration projects—bricks, stencils, spray paint, you get the idea. Anything else you want to say about marriage marriage marriage, and what we need instead?

GC: Donate Donate Donate! Do you have a moment for Prop 8? Do you have a moment for Prop 8? But really—we need to be able to choose our own families and who visits us in the hospital and who shares our assets and who makes decisions for us, whether we are officially single or partnered. And gender is defined by us too, not by presentation but how we define our own identities. Sexual liberation and freedom and places to fuck without being policed. Housing. Healthcare. Social services. Protection for the environment.

HG: The last time I checked—the nuclear family model—was a disaster! Enough already. The gay rights movement needs to divorce marriage and pull it together. The system is broken, these institutions are failing, why are people so set on shoring them up? Let's focus on ending capitalism, abolishing prison, ending militarism, ensuring immigrant rights, clean air, great food, love, equality, interdependence, independence, autonomy, non-hierarchical structures, and most importantly the universal reclamation of all land and water as public property.

YN: And, of course, the abolition of the prison industrial complex, the end of the illusion that more punishment and enhanced penalties in the form of hate crimes legislation will benefit anyone, safety for young queers who are beaten and/or raped by families and have nowhere to go, intergenerational sex that's not immediately stigmatized as pedophilia, an end to sex offender laws that do nothing to end the abuse of children but only add to the coffers of the prison industrial complex, an end to the death penalty, an end to the idea that life without parole is an acceptable alternative, queer sex in public without paying a fee in a bathhouse and without being harassed, jailed, or beaten for it, an immigration rights movement that acknowledges that it's a crisis of labor, not about "families" or spousal partners, an end to the disappearance and/or deportation of undocumented people, and oh, I could go on.

There's this popular line going around about how gay marriage is the rising tide that will lift all boats. But if we are to use a seafaring metaphor, it might be more apt to call it a Titanic, doomed to crash into an iceberg and take the rest of us down.

About the Authors

Mattilda Bernstein Sycamore is most recently the author of *So Many Ways to Sleep Badly* (City Lights 2008), and the editor of *Nobody Passes: Rejecting the Rules of Gender and Conformity* (Seal 2007) and an expanded second edition of *That's Revolting! Queer Strategies for Resisting Assimilation* (Soft Skull 2008). Mattilda recently finished a new anthology, *Why Are Faggots So Afraid of Faggots?: Flaming Challenges to Masculinity, Objectification and the Desire to Conform*, and is working on a public art project called Lostmissing and a memoirish thing called *The End of San Francisco*. She loves feedback. (www.mattildabernsteinsycamore.com)

Kate Borstein is an author, playwright and performance artist whose work to date has been in service to sex positivity and gender anarchy. Her work on behalf of building a coalition of those who live on cultural margins recently earned her an award from the Stonewall Democrats of New York City, as well as two citations from New York City Council members. Kate's latest book, *Hello, Cruel World: 101 Alternatives To Suicide For Teens, Freaks, and Other Outlaws*, was published in 2007. According to daily email and Twitter, the book is still helping people stay alive. Other published works include the books *Gender Outlaw: On Men, Women and the Rest of Us*, and *My Gender Workbook*. Kate's books are taught in over 150 colleges around the world. Her memoir, *Kate Bornstein Is A Queer and Pleasant Danger* is due out from Seven Stories Press in April, 2011.

Ryan Conrad is an outlaw artist, terrorist academic, petty thief from a small mill town in Maine. He works through visual culture and performance to rupture the queer here and now in hopes of making time and space to imagine the most fantastic queer futures. His visual work is archived at www.faggotz.org and he is a member of the editorial collective for *Against Equality*. He can be reached at rconrad@meca.edu.

John D'Emilio has been a pioneer in the developing field of gay and lesbian studies. He is the author or editor of more than half a dozen books, including *Sexual Politics, Sexual Communities: the Making of a Homosexual Minority in the United States*; *Intimate Matters: A History of Sexuality in America* [with Estelle Freedman]; and *Lost Prophet: The Life and Times of Bayard Rustin*. His essay, "Capitalism and Gay Identity," first printed in 1983, still gets reprinted almost three decades later. D'Emilio has won fellowships from the Guggenheim Foundation and the National Endowment for the Humanities; was a finalist for the National Book Award; and received the Brudner Prize from Yale University for lifetime contributions to gay and lesbian studies. A former co-chair of the board of directors of the National Gay and Lesbian Task Force, he was also the founding director of its Policy Institute. *Intimate Matters* was quoted by Supreme Court Associate Justice Anthony Kennedy in the 2003 *Lawrence v. Texas* case, the decision that declared state sodomy statutes unconstitutional. When not working, he watches old movies, solves sudoku puzzles, and searches for New York style pizza in Chicago.

Kenyon Farrow is the Executive Director of Queers for Economic Justice, an organization that does community organizing, leadership development, research and advocacy with, and on issues that impact, low-income and working class LGBTQ people. As a writer, Kenyon is a regular contributor to TheGrio.com. He is also the co-editor of Letters from *Young Activists: Today's Rebels Speak Out* (Nation Books), and the forthcoming *Stand Up!: The Politics of Racial Uplift* (South End Press).

Martha Jane Kaufman is a playwright, dancer and teacher. She has received awards and commissions from the San Francisco Playwrights' Foundation, the National Foundation for Advancement in the Arts, and Young Playwrights Inc. Her dances have been performed in theaters, galleries, elevators, stairwells and on street corners from Oakland, CA to Northampton MA, to Novi Sad, Serbia. She is currently a playwriting fellow at the Huntington Theatre and a member of the Royal Frog Ballet Performance Collective.

Katie Miles lives in Brooklyn, New York, where she works as a nanny. She is an activist who works on issues of economic justice, gentrification and displacement. She was raised in San Francisco

Yasmin Nair is a Chicago-based writer, activist, academic, and commentator, and a member of the Against Equality collective. The bastard child of queer theory and deconstruction, Nair's work has appe... publications like *GLQ*, *make/shift*, *The Bilerico Project*, *Windy City Times*, *Bitch*, *Maximum Rock'n'Roll*, and *No More Potlucks*. Nair is well known—and either loved or hated, depending on whom you ask—for her critiques of a ridiculous gay movement which pretends that the right to marry, the right to kill as part of the U.S. war machine, and hate crimes legislation actually constitute some kind of leftist agenda. She is a member of the Chicago grassroots organization Gender JUST (Justice United for Societal Transformation). Nair is currently working on a book about affect and neoliberalism, tentatively titled *Feeling Bad*. Her website is at www.yasminnair.net

Kate Raphael has been a radical queer activist for over 25 years. She is a cofounder of QUIT! Queers Undermining Israeli Terrorism and a member of LAGAI-Queer Insurrection, one of the oldest anti-assimilationist queer groups in the world. She spent over a month in Israeli jails for her work supporting Palestinian nonviolent resistance, and is a former grand marshal of the San Francisco LGBT Pride Parade.

Dean Spade is the founder of the Sylvia Rivera Law Project (www.srlp.org), a non-profit law collective providing free legal help to trans people of color and low income people and working to build racial and economic justice centered trans resistance. He is also an assistant professor at Seattle University School of Law teaching poverty law, law and social movements, and critical perspectives on transgender law.

Eric a Stanley was kicked out of high school at the age of 14 and is currently a PhD. candidate in the History of Consciousness program at UCSC. Among the collectives that keep Eric busy are Gay Shame SF and Critical Resistance. Along with Chris Vargas, Eric directed *Homotopia* and *Criminal Queers*. Eric is also working on editing the first ever trans/queer prison studies anthology with Nat Smith called *Captive Genders: Trans Embodiment and the Prison Industrial Complex* (forthcoming AK Press).

Craig Willse is a writer, activist , and teacher. He is a doctoral student in sociology at the Graduate Center, City University of New York, where he is working on a dissertation about technoscience, race, and economies of population management. Craig's writing has appeared in *Economy and Society*, *Widener Law Review*, and the *Journal of Aesthetics and Protest*. His other interests include bikes, complexity theory, DIY artificial insemination, Tucson, talking to artists, farms, farmers, and thinking critically about the academic industrial complex. Craig plays keyboards in the pop band The Ballet, who recently self-released their second album, Bear Life.

Deeg is a fat butch lesbian who lives in the SF Bay Area. Deeg has been working as an anti-assimilation, queer liberation activist for about 40 years, and believes that the liberation struggle must include fighting against all forms of oppression. Deeg is a member of LAGAI—Queer Insurrection, which has been fighting against imperialism, racisim, sexism, and all other bad things since 1983, and is also a member of Queers Undermining Israeli Terrorism (QUIT!). Both LAGAI and QUIT! believe that we need to create a just and free world in which people can be happy, rather than seek "equality" in this wretched straight society.